VERILY

SPAM TOMORROW

VERILY ANDERSON was born Verily Bruce in 1915. Though she published more than 30 books – memoirs, biographies, children's stories and work ranging from personal reminiscences to Shakespeare scholarship – her breakthrough as a writer came in 1956 when she published *Spam Tomorrow*, the classic account of her wartime experiences on the home front. Elizabeth Bowen hailed it as a new kind of memoir, one of the first to explore the lives of women in wartime.

During the war she met Donald Anderson. They married in 1940 and had five children. Donald died in 1956, and for the remainder of her life Verily worked primarily as a writer. When Verily married architect Paul Paget in 1971, Joyce Grenfell was matron of honour, and John Betjeman best man.

Her last book – a memoir of the time she spent at Herstmonceux Castle, Sussex, in the 1930s and 40s – was completed the day before she died.

Verily Anderson died in 2010, at the age of ninety-five. She was survived by four children, sixteen grandchildren, fourteen great-grandchildren – and Alfie, her beloved RNIB guide-dog.

WORKS BY VERILY ANDERSON

Memoir

Spam Tomorrow (1956)
Our Square (1957)
Beware of Children (1958)
Daughters of Divinity (1960)
The Flo Affair (1963)
Scrambled Egg for Christmas (1970)

Children's Fiction

The Brownie Series
Amanda and the Brownies (1960)
The Brownies and the Golden Hand (1963)
The Brownies' Day Abroad (1964)
The Brownies and the Ponies (1965)
Brownies on Wheels (1966)
The Brownies and Their Animal Friends (1969)
The Brownie Cookbook (1974)
The Brownies and the Wedding Day (1974)
The Camp Fire Book (1976)
The Brownies and the Christening (1977)

The Yorks Series
Vanload to Venice (1961)
Nine Times Never (1962)
The Yorks in London (1964)

Non-Series
Clover Cloverdale (1974)

Non-Fiction

The Northrepps Grandchildren (1968)
The Last of the Eccentrics: A Life of Rosslyn Bruce (1972)
Friends and Relations: Three Centuries of Quaker Families (1980)
The De Veres of Castle Hedingham (1993)
Castellans of Herstmonceux (1911-2010) (2011)

VERILY ANDERSON

SPAM TOMORROW

With an introduction by
Rachel Anderson

DEAN STREET PRESS

A Furrowed Middlebrow Book
FM32

Published by Dean Street Press 2019

First published in 1956 by Rupert Hart-Davis

Cover by DSP

ISBN 978 1 913054 21 2

www.deanstreetpress.co.uk

TO PAM & JIM ROSE

INTRODUCTION

SHE WAS NAMED by her father, a country parson, as an aide-mémoire for those proverbs of Jesus which begin, 'Verily, verily I say unto you—' Believing they'd misheard, strangers frequently referred to her as Verity or Valerie. She rarely took offence, insisting, 'It is an offence to take offence.'

At four, she began writing stories and poems, also plays for her youngest sister to perform. After a haphazard education, chiefly at home with her mother, she showed considerable musical talent and at 16 was accepted to study at the Royal College of Music. However, when it became evident that she'd not make a concert pianist, her father stopped paying the fees. So she began to earn her living as a mechanic, chauffeur, nursemaid, designer of toffee papers, advertising copywriter, and sub-editing the Girl Guides' magazine, *The Guide*. And, despite rejections, she continued to write her own stories.

In 1939 she enlisted with the FANY's (First Aid Nursing Yeomanry) on the grounds that if there were to be a war, 'it would be less frightening to be in the middle of things'. In 1940 she married Donald Anderson, playwright and veteran soldier of WW1.

After the war, they supported themselves, and their increasing number of children, as freelance writers, he specialising in military history, she as a talent scout for a film company while simultaneously editing *The Townsend,* the monthly magazine of the Girls Friendly Society, the Christian-based organisation that offered young women both spiritual and practical encouragement. When short of copy to fill the magazine's pages, Verily encouraged friends and neighbours to contribute whatever they could in the way of news items, poems, lyrics, illustrations. Verily also persuaded well-known writers of the time, including Enid Blyton, Marghanita Laski, Noel Streatfeild, to donate stories. Under a pseudonym, Verily produced the monthly serial,

Clover Coverdale. Years later, Verily's narrative demonstrating the inner courage a young girl must find to survive conflagration, devastation, loss of family members, was published under her own name as a teenage novel.

In 1954, in an emotionally charged farewell editorial for *The Townsend,* she wrote, 'The war took so much from us that we grew to accept deprivations almost without feeling. We lost friends, we lost our homes, we lost whole ways of life. . . . (yet) we learned that, even in the parting of death, something of the spirit is left behind on earth, something that we had perhaps not known to exist in the living person, something that had lain dormant as the hidden seeds of the willow-herb in the sooty City of London.'

Within weeks of giving up editorship of *The Townsend*, she began turning her first-hand war experiences into a book.

From the age of nine, she kept a daily diary, of which there remain 142 volumes, all marked 'Strictly Private'. These were never intended for public reading, let alone publication. However, the war-time volumes, 1939-1945, were almost certainly the catalyst for *Spam Tomorrow.*

She finished the first draft in six weeks.

Publication was an unexpected success. Elizabeth Bowen, the Irish novelist, wrote, 'This is a genuinely bizarre book. This author has had the good idea of writing about a new kind of wartime experience – new, that is, to literature; the job of marrying and having babies. . . . Those who agree with it will become incurable addicts.'

There followed serialisations in popular magazines, and numerous readers' letters responding to this authentic account of women's everyday WW2 lives. The Imperial War Museum requested a copy for their archive. And a younger generation of women writing about wartime London have turned to *Spam* for reference.

Donald Anderson died within a year of publication. Verily's profound sorrow is revealed in the dedication to her third book, *Beware of Children*:

TO MY IMMORTAL.

One noisy night in the Blitz, he said, "Stick by me, darling, and we'll both be all right. I'm immortal."
And he is.

However, with five children aged from three to 15, as well as her own widowed mother to care for, Verily could not succumb to a Queen Victoria-style of widow's grief. She carried on with magazine journalism, lectures, school visits, and books for all ages, earning just enough to get by.

In her late 50s when her children had reached adulthood, she married for the second time. Now, supported by her new husband, she was able to give up the pot-boilers and journalism to complete the biography of her father, Reverend Doctor Rosslyn Bruce, fox-hunting, terrier-breeding humanitarian rector.

Janet Adam Smith, the biographer, concluded her review of *The Last of the Eccentrics,* 'Verily Anderson goes to her work with zest. . . . She leaves one with a great sense of a living person, vital, warm and free . . . whose high spirits were the consequences not of ignoring the dark and painful but of conviction for the reality of goodness and love. '

This summing-up of Rosslyn Bruce's life could equally well be a summary of Verily's own long and vigorously loving life.

As Verily's eye-sight began to fade, her piano was moved next to her bedroom to be more easily reached and she took to dictating her work, leaving her family to correct it. On being registered blind, she insisted, with typical positivity, how delighted she was that at last she qualified to be trained for a guide-dog. She then dictated an article for *The Author* (Society of Authors journal) discussing how Milton might have adapted to having a canine carer.

Her final book, which was published posthumously, is a memoir of the residents of the 15th century castle which lay within her father's parish. In 1947 Herstmonceux became the site of the Royal Greenwich Observatory, and is currently the Bader International Study Centre for Queen's University, Ontario, Canada.

Verily died in her sleep two days after completing the text for *Castellans of Herstmonceux* with her guide-dog at her bedside. She was ninety-five and a half.

Rachel Anderson
Northrepps

"LONG-DISTANCE call for Bruce," a F.A.N.Y. sergeant, soured by the years of peace between the wars, looked into the common-room and addressed me in the third person. "It can be taken in the office but must be short. Personal calls are not encouraged during a state of emergency."

The state of emergency had been present for two months, at any rate in our unit, since the evacuation from Dunkirk.

I zipped up my khaki skirt, loosened after lunch, and ran to the telephone. It might be Donald. It was.

"What size do you take in wedding rings?" his voice asked from London.

"I don't know, darling. Why? Are we going to be married?"

"That's what I should like. Can you get leave?"

"Of course, darling." I would have married Donald any time he asked me since I first met him a few years before.

"What about tomorrow?"

"All right, darling. Of course."

"Bruce," the voice at my elbow interrupted, "you're on the duty list."

"Good-bye," I said rather stiffly into the telephone.

"Till tomorrow then, my love," I heard. The sergeant was eyeing my lack of a collar-stud sharply. I replaced the receiver reluctantly.

"Utility van CZ404," said the sergeant. "Pick up Captain Bland at the depot and drive him to Birmingham. Here are your orders." She handed me a slip.

So much for my quiet afternoon in the town finding out what size I took in wedding rings. So much for my quickly made plan to catch the C.O. in a mellow mood and ask for leave.

I had joined the First Aid Nursing Yeomanry, which has supplied drivers of army vehicles—horse and otherwise—since the Boer War, in a burst of mixed patriotism and fear soon after

Munich. Three days before war was declared I was recalled from my holiday abroad to sit about in a variety of F.A.N.Y. common-rooms all over the country, kicking my heels and asking for trouble. Everywhere there were too few vehicles and too many F.A.N.Y. drivers. Days would pass before your turn came round to drive, or even maintain, an unconverted furniture van or borrowed limousine. I suppose conditions were much the same in the real army at the time, but somehow our amateurishness made them seem to be our fault.

Utility van CZ404 had been oiled and greased by an over-ardent F.A.N.Y., obviously delighted to be allowed to do it. There was grease on the steering-wheel and oil on the seats. I warned Captain Bland, a fair, shy young man, to look out for his trousers as he got in. He blushed, misunderstanding me.

Birmingham was thirty miles away. He was not inclined to talk. Nor was I. I had my dreams to play with.

In Birmingham Captain Bland only kept me waiting a few minutes. On the way out I made a detour partly to avoid the tram-lines, and partly so that I could see the street where I was born. As we had left that house when I was seven, the street naturally now looked shorter and the houses smaller than I remembered. I generalised about this kind of thing to Captain Bland.

"Oh? So you're a midlander?" he looked relieved.

"Only born. I was brought up in the south."

A look of mistrust returned to his eyes. We passed a jeweller's shop against whose window I had often pressed my nose during nursery walks with the pram. I remembered my delight in the glitter of the grown ups' toys, and how I had filled the palaces of my imagination with chiming clocks and precious stones.

I pulled up outside the shop.

"I won't be a minute," I said to Captain Bland, pocketing the ignition key and going into the shop.

"Could you tell me what size I take in rings?" I asked the man standing behind the glass-topped counter.

He produced a set of metal plates hinged together, rather like the gadget we had been instructed in M.T. lectures to use for measuring fractions of an inch when reseating a sparking plug.

"Try your finger in some of these holes, madam," said the man.

I offered the third finger of my left hand.

"Are you interested in engagement rings?" he asked. "We have a splendid selection."

"No thank you," I said, realising that Donald and I would have no time for such frills as an engagement if we were to be married tomorrow.

"Your size in rings is P," said the assistant courteously.

"P," I repeated, thanking him. I hurried into the post office, which I remembered lay at the back of a grocer's two shops away. I wrote out a telegram to Donald saying: "P DARLING STOP YOUR ADORING V."

I turned to find Captain Bland at my elbow reading what I had written.

"I say," he said, blushing. "Isn't this rather irregular?"

"I'll tell you about it in the van," I said.

"But I don't think I ought to let you send that telegram."

"It's all right," I said gently, as though soothing a frightened child. "I'm not a fifth columnist. It's just I'm going to be married tomorrow, and my—" I couldn't bring myself to pronounce the unfamiliar word fiancé "—the man I'm going to marry wants to buy a wedding ring."

"Oh," Captain Bland blushed and slunk back to the van.

As we drove along I managed to convince him that he had not failed in his duty.

"You F.A.N.Y.s are an odd lot," he volunteered.

"Unconventional at times," I agreed, "but see how we get things done." I couldn't think quite what things I had got done in nearly a year's active service, but was sure other F.A.N.Y.s in other places had.

"I don't think you're a fifth columnist," Captain Bland said presently.

"Thank you."

When I set him down at the depot he blushed in every visible place and then turned back to say, "Good luck."

The C.O. refused to give me forty-eight hours' leave. The best I could get was a couple of hours off to go and buy a hair-net. My hair, she said, was not actually on my collar but was the kind that looked as though it was. It would be better in a net.

I was sick of the subject of my hair. All my life it had been a trial to me. When I was a little girl, strangers would stop my mother and embarrass me by saying how beautiful it was. This incited my mother to brush it up from underneath more than ever, to produce an even fluffier effect of curls. "Verily Bruce, when did you last brush your hair?" echoed through my school days, even when I had tugged away with a brush and comb long after everybody else had begun breakfast. Now in the F.A.N.Y.s this kind of thing had begun again.

I did not buy a hair-net. Instead I took a bus to a cousin's house in the country where I often went when local leave only was offered.

"You look pale," said Aunt Evie over tea, "not yourself at all."

"I know," I said truthfully. "I don't feel myself."

"I'm not going to let you go back to those draughty camp-beds looking like that," she said firmly. "Beryl," she turned to her younger niece, "telephone Verily's young woman and tell her I'm keeping her for the night. If she starts to argue, tell her I used to know her father. A rotten bad shot he was too."

Tall, pretty Beryl wandered away to shatter, in her gentle caressing voice, the discipline of my unit.

My cousin Peter wanted to know all about what went on in the F.A.N.Y.s. I tried to explain in such military terms as I had picked up; but it was impossible to take the corps seriously with Peter—of the Grenadier Guards—making so light of the war proper, his Dunkirk wounds still encased in plaster.

During dinner the ancient parlour-maid, retrieved from retirement for the duration, handed Beryl a telegram.

"Beryl's instant recall to the quarter-deck," Peter suggested. "The navy can't put to sea without her."

"The navy doesn't even know I'm joining it yet," said Beryl, opening the telegram. She read it and burst out laughing. "Medieval pub!" she quoted. "What can it mean?" She turned over the envelope. "Oh, how silly of me! It's for you, Verily. It's been forwarded from the F.A.N.Y.s."

"Verily Bruce—Beryly Bruce—a natural confusion," observed Peter.

I took the telegram and read, "Double room facing south booked medieval pub." The time showed it had been sent off soon after Donald's telephone call to me.

I could feel Peter's eyebrows raised waiting for an explanation of the "medieval pub". I looked wildly round for a cue to something to say. The ancestors on the walls, most of them guilty of raffish deeds at some time or another, looked down with amusement, but offered no help.

By a wonderful piece of luck Uncle Percy suddenly began to choke over a crumb—or perhaps it was deliberate diplomacy. I had managed to hold Uncle Percy's sympathy ever since I was five, when he agreed that I was right to put a fellow bridesmaid in an empty water-butt.

"Why not go the whole hog and have a fit?" Peter said in the cheeky and affectionate manner he used for addressing his father. He got up casually and patted his father's back with his good arm.

"All right," Uncle Percy gasped, before he had recovered. "I'll try."

"Don't talk," Aunt Evie pressed him; "it only makes it worse."

Beryl and I hastened to Uncle Percy's side with glasses of water, entangling ourselves with three dogs on the way.

In the excitement the telegram was forgotten.

That evening I undressed in Beryl's room so that we could talk secrets, as we used to do when we were little girls. Beryl could hardly wait to hear about the double room facing south.

"It must be for our honeymoon," I said thoughtfully, putting on the pyjamas I had borrowed from Beryl. I told her about Donald and how I hoped to marry him tomorrow.

"Do the family know?" She was most intrigued.

"They've met him. They don't think he's suitable."

"Why? Is he divorced?"

Beryl's blue eyes looked even bigger than usual.

"Good heavens, no! It's just he's hopeless at making any money. But he's terribly sweet. Only he's never thought he was suitable either," I sighed.

"But he does now?"

"He must do. I suppose the steady job he's got at the Ministry makes him suitable. He came out of the regular army before the war to write a West End success."

"And was it?"

"Not quite West End, but he wrote some beautiful poetry."

"Not a very practical man?"

"Oh, I wouldn't say that. You have to be practical to write poetry, let alone producible plays. It's just he's not a very good business man."

Beryl was sitting on the window-sill with her chin resting on her knees.

"What are you going to wear?"

"When?"

"Tomorrow. Not a very practical girl. I can see why your family think the idea unsuitable."

"Oh, tomorrow? I hadn't thought. Uniform, I suppose."

"Darling, you can't." Beryl could be firm in her own vague way. "Uniform's much too unromantic for your sort of marriage."

"It's all I've got here."

"I'm going to buy you something tomorrow before you go to London. You can't go back to the F.A.N.Y.s. This is much too important."

"I suppose I'm deserting," I said.

"Does it matter?"

"I don't think so. They won't want to shoot me or anything. I'm not much use to them. Just another mouth to feed."

Aunt Evie was horrified when she heard next morning what I intended to do.

"What will your parents think of me!" she said. "They'll think I was aiding and abetting you. I wish I'd known nothing about it."

I said good-bye to Beryl at the railway station, clutching the trousseau she had so generously bought me, together with a satin-and-lace nightgown which Aunt Evie bought me on the strict understanding that she had nothing more to do with the mad adventure.

At the ticket office I asked for a single to London, but discovered that, without a C.O.'s leave pass, members of the services were being refused railway tickets. So the state of emergency was not confining itself to our unit.

I wandered into the nearest hotel and sat down to think what to do next. I could change into the mufti Beryl had given me and wait until another ticket clerk came on duty. I could go back to my C.O. and beg for compassionate leave. Or I could listen to the voice of reason and postpone the whole thing and wait until the state of emergency ended, either in enemy invasion or not.

Outside in the street I could see a young man in wavy-navy uniform parking a big sports car. He came into the hotel, passing me on his way to the cocktail bar. Somewhere in the dim past I had seen him before. The sports car opened up new possibilities.

I followed him into the cocktail bar, ordered a drink, and took a chance.

"Weren't you at school with my brother Merlin?" I asked him.

"Merlin Bruce? Yes. Which sister are you?"

"Verily."

"Have a drink."

"I've got one, thank you." We settled down to talk old times. Tomorrow, he told me, his leave ended and he was driving back to London before he rejoined his ship. He agreed to pick me up at the hotel after breakfast.

I telephoned Donald, who told me he had bought a marriage licence from the Archbishop of Canterbury with a wonderful seal dangling from it, like Magna Carta.

Then I booked a room in the hotel and washed my hair. When it was dry I went downstairs for a meal, but was quickly driven back by the sight of half a dozen F.A.N.Y. officers from my unit with their escorts. I sat in my room till hunger drove me down the fire-escape to a nearby fish-and-chip shop. I felt like the bad girl of a school story as I sneaked up again in the dark. In my present mood, I suppose I would have knotted my sheets and climbed down them if there had been no fire-escape.

At the appointed hour next day I waited outside the hotel for Miles and his sports car. I was not at all certain that he would remember his ready offer of the day before, so I was very relieved when a series of explosions and wisps of blue smoke showed that he had.

"Leap in," he said affably.

At his first stop of many for petrol, oil, and several adjust-ments to the engine, I spent the last of my pay on a scarf to protect my newly washed hair from the smoke which poured up from under the floor-boards.

It was an extraordinary car. It seemed to have no happy medium between roaring along at seventy miles an hour and stopping dead, with one wheel leaning slightly inwards in a position which, viewed from the road, had a perplexed air about it. Miles seemed to have little control over which pace it chose. The journey was made even longer by the number of friends he knew on, or slightly off, the route. It was soon fairly clear that I should not reach London in time to be married that day. In fact

Miles began to wonder whether it was really necessary for me to marry at all.

"Seems an awful waste," he said, "a girl like you getting hitched up like that. Think of all the fun you'll miss."

At eight o'clock in the evening the car roared up Piccadilly, and with some difficulty Miles brought her alongside just before Half Moon Street as Donald strolled out of his club, with the marriage licence in his hand and the wedding ring, size P, in his pocket.

Before I had time to thank Miles properly, his car seemed to spring away out of his hands, and Piccadilly was temporarily hidden in blue fog.

"Hallo, darling," said Donald, kissing me as though I had just got off a number 9 bus from Knightsbridge, instead of having been hurled a hundred and fifty miles through a smoke screen. "Lorema's in the club."

Lorema is my youngest sister and she had always found Donald less unsuitable than the rest of the family imagined him. I was glad she was there. She was delighted with Beryl's choice of clothes for me and decided that she too must dress up for the wedding, which was now timed for two o'clock the next day. To dress Lorema up, she and I had to take a taxi to a cousin's house in Chelsea, put a ladder on the roof of the taxi up to the window of the room where Lorema had left her finery while the cousin was away, and climb up through the window to collect two suitcases. Such was the innocence of our approach that the taxi-driver was satisfied we were not house-breakers.

Lorema and I spent that night with the parents of Elizabeth, my truest F.A.N.Y. friend. The last time I had been in that house was for Elizabeth's wedding, when all her family and friends were round her.

Suddenly I decided to telephone my parents and ask them to come to our wedding. My mother was very annoyed, indeed it was out of fear of her disapproval that we had kept our plans from her. Now she tried to stop the wedding. If I got married today she would—she started to use an old threat reaching back to the school-room—stop my pocket money. She never wanted to see me again and, anyway, where were we going for our honeymoon? I told her the name of the country inn where Donald had arranged for us to spend the week-end. She banged down the receiver.

Yes, this was love all right.

2

THEY SAY that the life of a drowning man unrolls before him as his end approaches. Marriage, too, seemed to me to mark an end as well as a beginning. Perhaps that is why my life unrolled before me when I stood as a bride at the altar of the church in Down Street, Mayfair.

I was intensely conscious of the seriousness of the vows of the marriage ceremony; but at the same time my youth sprang up with a clarity such as I never before remembered. I wondered whether Donald too was seeing his longer and more varied life in the same way; or does the change to the married state only affect a female with such a sense of finality?

My earliest memory was of tearing a bandage from my eye after an operation. I was two. Some of the tall people known in the nursery as "they"—mother, nurse, maids, and even older children—then tied my hands behind my back while another bandage was bound over my eye. But, in spite of this and other just as unattractive memories, on my fourth birthday I looked back over my life, as I did now at my wedding, and decided it had been good; so good that I hoped to be allowed in heaven to live it again and again, at least eight times, cutting out the bandages and all spankings and naughtiness; then, once only, to live it exactly as it had been, complete with misfortunes.

Part of my glorious infancy was spent at my maternal grand-mother's in Norfolk. Ecstatic was my joy as I ran round the little formal paths at Northrepps between the low box-hedges divid-ing beds of geraniums from forget-me-nots. The sensation of rolling down velvety mown slopes stayed with me for months after we returned to Birmingham for the winter. Summer after summer I would search in the Northrepps woods for the elusive clearing where my companions—boy cousins and a brother all about a year older than myself—built our first hut of branches, in which we ate shrimps netted by ourselves at Overstrand, the shore within donkey-cart distance. How the shrimps turned pink and edible while we left them in a bucket of sea-water in the nursery was a mystery to me. When our nurses got together, they always shared some secret joke against us; and I suspected that they might have tampered with our shrimps.

About my father's side of the family there hung for me an air of unpredictable variety. Sometimes pictures of them were pointed out in history books or public buildings or racy weekly papers. Members of my mother's family were in history books too, but only for worthy causes.

My father is a parson. He has bred smooth fox terriers since the age of six. His effervescent friendliness and ten-minute sermons took him several times round the United States; he judged at dog shows as he went. He walks with a limp from breaking his leg out hunting. This led to his meeting my mother as he lay recovering in a friend's house in Norfolk. My mother quickly took him into her parents' home, where she nursed him by taking his crutches away and standing just out of reach. Photographs show that she was very pretty. They were married when she was twenty-two.

One of my father's interests is words. He devised a system for naming his five children. Each name had to have six letters; and, because his and my mother's names contain an R and an L, each of ours had to too—plus some peculiarity not shared by others. *Merlin* (n), *Rhalou* (h), *Erroll* (doubles), *Verily* (v)—not so much a name as an adverb—and finally, to fall in with the system, he had to invent *Lorema*. Lorema had flaxen curls and the face of a naughty angel.

When we left Birmingham, my father was given one of the most beautiful livings in southern England, with the Sussex downs rolling away to the west and the sea sparkling to the south, beyond marshes and wooded glebe. It was a splendid place in which to bring up a family. Merlin and Erroll, who both went in the navy later, had their first experience of navigation on the rectory pond, where we all learned to swim along with the ducks. We rode fat uncomfortable ponies, lent to my father in exchange for their grazing. We were taught to shoot with my father's highly dangerous old hammer gun. Why we never lost limbs or our lives is hard to understand. But all our accidents were mild; and death seldom came within our ken.

Although a parson, my father has never liked to dwell on death. Even the animals, as they grew old, were hustled away to die elsewhere. So, as a little girl, loving life as I did and finding simple questions about death evaded, I became obsessed by the subject. I noticed that the bones of dead birds remained long in the fields.

"How much of Mrs. Honeysett will rot in her coffin?" I asked with some interest, when my father mentioned at lunch that he had buried her that morning. I was gently rebuffed.

"Could you dig her up soon to see?" I pressed on.

* * * * *

One summer night there came a thunderstorm so terrible that my teeth chattered as I lay in bed, and the telephone bell rang in short pings as lightning struck the wires. Then came a long insistent ring. I heard my parents discuss the necessity of answering it. My father went downstairs to the telephone. I could hear his voice sink to the pitch that he reserves for certain parts of the church services.

He came upstairs and I heard him talk again to my mother, still in this special voice. My mother's was clearer. She would wake one of the maids to stay with the children, she said, then she would dress as quickly as she could. She supposed the car would start in such a storm, she added doubtfully. The car was new and only she could drive it.

The telephone rang out clearly again. My father went down to it. Between the crashes of thunder overhead, I listened to the rustle of my mother dressing. Then my father returned and said, "It was the police again. Too late. He's dead. It was a terrible fall."

They went back to bed.

The storm raged on: but now it was a fear of something much greater and more awful than thunder and lightning that kept me awake.

I went to my mother's room.

"Who fell and died?" I asked in the darkness.

"Just one of your father's cousins," my mother said sleepily, as though it was only to be expected of them.

Next morning I said nothing, but I overheard enough through the subdued bustle that went on to know that it was Beryl's father—Uncle Percy's twin, and a great dear in my opinion—who had been killed in a strange accident, while watching the freak storm from the promenade at Eastbourne, where he was staying.

He was buried in our churchyard while Beryl, tiny and sweet in white muslin threaded with black ribbons, had a dolls' tea-party with me under the nursery table. I had planned it reverently on a sober note; but soon it was clear that Beryl, crawling out for a quick dance by herself, had no idea of the solemnity of death.

"This is a Highland fling my daddy's teaching me because his regiment is a little bit Scotch," she said, and floated about again. She was like a flower.

I sat alone under the table, terrified now for her—of what she would feel when she found out that her father was dead.

The chief interest of the heartless public seemed to be that Beryl's little brother inherited his father's title before he was six.

It was weeks before Beryl knew. Then at first she was rather relieved. Associating his disappearance with the arrival of stern policemen, she had feared that he had been taken to prison.

* * * * *

Being the fourth in the family, I rarely had new clothes. Rhalou's smelt of the stables and kennels. I hated them. But Erroll's shoes and other unsexed garments were all right. Best of all were clothes that came in big parcels from a set of Bruce cousins, whose mother delighted in buying them pretty things and as quickly tired of them. I loved these cousins, as much for themselves as for their clothes; and, when we occasionally met, Nancy and Cherry and Rosemary and I formed secret societies, whose secrecy was well advertised by enormous volumes of noise. They were all younger than I, but two of them only just, so I was able to squeeze myself into sun-dresses they had worn at Cannes and the ski-ing clothes they wore at St. Moritz; and they fitted in places—though never more than only just.

* * * * *

My father maintains that our school bills were paid by the stud fees of the terriers he bred. And certainly there was never a week when the village carrier did not come lumbering down the drive bringing one or more boxed bitches to a dog's wedding.

In self-defence my mother has always kept a pekinese, to rollock behind her, jump into the car in the hopes of a ride, steal her chocolates, sleep on her bed, and give my father daily cause to decry its breed. House-dogs, he says, were never intended. Other house-animals must have been; for in his study, bare of curtains or carpets, he has always kept birds of many species, unusual colours in mice, and generally some oddity like a viper or an iguana. Religious prints, pale biscuit-coloured photographs of choirs at former livings, paintings of champion terriers, and one of his college at Oxford, all hang together between the bookshelves and crucifixes, with his badges of office in the Free-masons, Boys' Brigade, and Rotary. To an ordinary person it is a most uncomfortable room, and sometimes smells as strongly as the hippo house at the zoo.

A young writer who came to live in the village often sat in the study with my father playing chess or, with even more hilarity (for their chess was never silent), helping to compose a sacred verse. Norrie said of the study that he liked to feel it would eventually bring him nearer heaven, just by the very height of the smell.

We all adored Norrie, and made him try to skate on the frozen pond on one leg, for he lost the other in the first war. We persuaded him to climb a tree to see the hut we had built in it, without having first given a thought to how we should get him down again; and occasionally, to show our affection, we took a back wheel off his car before he left. His youthful cynicism had a refreshing influence on us all.

As far as the education of us girls was concerned, the terriers began by keeping a series of governesses, the first of whom left with an incurable headache caused by the howls of the terriers. The next governess agreed that dogs' barking was bad, not so much at feeding-times when they all barked, as in the night, when those poor lonely bitches would howl for the comfort, perhaps, of their own homes, or maybe just because marriage did not appeal to them. Sometimes Rhalou, who never had my fear of the dark, would go out in her pyjamas to bring a howler in. This led to her keeping ferrets in her room, which practice was only stopped after one bit the ankle of Rose (who had been in the family for years), when she carried in a can of hot water for washing.

Not that we did a great deal of washing. Water was scarce, particularly in the summer. Every drop had to be pumped by hand. "Twenty pumps each way" was a very usual punishment for quite small offences. Electricity and an electric pump reached the rectory long after the rest of the village had gone all-electric. Glad as I was to hear the water gushing into the tanks, and occasionally gushing out over the tops of them and through the bathroom ceiling if someone forgot to switch off the electric pump, I regretted the passing from the rectory of candles and paraffin lamps, with their soft warming glow.

We learned very little from our governesses. If hounds ran anywhere near, Rhalou would suddenly disappear out of the schoolroom window and not be seen again all day. This was not seriously discouraged, except by the governesses. One day, while Rhalou was following the hounds, I borrowed her "piece" and practised it on the drawing-room piano instead of my own. Next day I could play it recognisably enough to cause friction. She called it theft for anyone to play another's "piece" (anyway it was only *The Merry Peasant*). And when my mother claimed me as a musical genius and took my side, Rhalou refused ever to play the piano again, which was a pity, because she had a much better ear than I had.

In our teens we were sent to a magnificent boarding-school owned by a cousin of my mother. It had turrets and towers and terraces; it had azaleas and four square miles of rhododendrons; it had five long drives with lodges and wrought-iron gates; and the ballroom was big enough for a regimental ball. But there was no central heating, at any rate in our day. It had been built fifty years before by a railway earl at the peak of his wealth. True, he had built into it some extravagant form of heating; but it was reputed to use one of his railway-trucks of fuel a day to keep it going. For us, sponges and water left in our wash-basins at night were frozen in the morning. My hands never recovered their shape, lost through chilblains. But I developed a strange love for the place itself, which had nothing to do with the honour of the school, for which I had no respect.

All the other girls were either rich or very noble. We Bruces were there at cost-price merely to help make a good show of girls when prospective parents came to inspect the school. My mother tried to skimp on the expensive uniform by making mine at home, which got my clothes such names as the *Soup-Bowler*, the *Bird-Watcher's-Treat*, and *Any-Minute-Now-Dear*.

For some reason I behaved atrociously at school and was beaten by the headmistress with, appropriately enough, a piece of weeping-birch from a most beautiful tree on the lawn.

After my beating I looked out of the turret window, down on to the paved terrace below, and decided against jumping out. I wonder what effect it would have had on my bruised emotions had I known that twenty years later I should be standing on the spot which I might have crashed on to, looking at an insignificant scar on the pine-topped hill, which was all that remained of our school after it was blown up as not being worth repairing.

The beating was for general naughtiness. I now think this must have been caused by the, to me, awful frustration of never for one minute of the day being allowed to do things of my own choice. I wanted to choose for myself which hour of the week I wrote home or experimented with scissors and glue. And, being a natural rebel, I chose.

Really bad sins, and—apart from my general naughtiness—mine seemed to be many, had to be owned up to before the whole school at prayers. As the headmistress read the register each girl stood up to announce her presence and to confess what she had done. So at prayers could be heard:

"Myrtale Bridgwater."

A scraping of shoes as Myrtale dragged her sturdy form to its feet.

"Present."

"Verily Bruce."

"Present. One conduct mark."

"What for?" asked the headmistress, who above everyone else knew the answer, for only she could give a conduct mark.

"For cutting up my knicker-linings to make a morse code flag."

"I told you to say for Calculated Destruction. Take another."

Sometimes it would be Myrtale who had the conduct mark; and my embarrassment for her or anyone else in the same predicament was as great as when I was the culprit.

Rhalou managed to become a prefect. But I was never more than a sub-prefect; and then I was reduced to the ranks for using my authority to force my dormitory to curl their hair with lavatory paper.

My only claims to success were in music and swimming. The music at school, so I discovered later, was poor; and I, having started off by stealing Rhalou's piece, did not find it difficult to work up to carrying off the music cup, which anyway was only given to the pupil showing the greatest improvement, and I had the room. The swimming cup was quite a different matter.

The first heats of the competition were held in the nearest town's swimming-bath. I was lucky enough to be in the last heat. The winners of the earlier ones were by now in the sanatorium with pink-eye, caught, it was believed, at the swimming-bath. So the next heats were held in the sea. It was rough and excruciatingly cold. Only the better-covered competitors would venture in. On the day of the final, waves were breaking over the promenade; so we were shepherded back into our bus, which the headmistress ordered to be driven to the ornamental lakes lying in the pine-woods below the school. It was common knowledge that these lakes were formed out of our waste bath-water, so there was a further falling off in competitors. But bath-water was nothing to one brought up to swim with ducks. Diving for a saucer in the mud was routine work for me, and I won the cup.

After school, as I was still spectacularly lacking in polish, it was decided to send me to Paris. Most girls from our school went to Paris for polish; though Rhalou had gone to America instead, to accompany my father on a Rotary Club tour.

One of our many French holiday governesses was more popular with us than most: and when she announced her engagement to an English schoolmaster we all set about making great plans for the wedding. We girls were to be bridesmaids, and Merlin, then a sub-lieutenant in the Navy, was to give her away. Merlin had been flirting with Jeanette harmlessly since he was twelve. At the last minute my mother had a brilliant idea for getting me to Paris without having to take me herself. I could go with the bridal couple.

Jeanette was quite amenable to this suggestion, but I think it must have been kept from the bridegroom.

The wedding went off gaily enough. My father officiated in the village church and the reception was held at the rectory. Afterwards the bride and bridegroom were hallooed away with a shoe tied on their car, which was hotly followed by Merlin and myself in his ramshackle old round-nosed Morris. Merlin had been learning to fly and, as we fell further and further behind, he decided to abandon the Morris when we reached his flying-club, and continue by air. I hated flying, particularly in small home-made-looking aircraft piloted by Merlin. But I had to pretend to like it. He had already taken us all up several times, looped the loop with us, and once, in a dual-control Avro, made Erroll and me take over in the air. The goat and my mother's pekinese also looped the loop; and it only remained for my mother to be forced off the earth by Merlin's enthusiasm.

Now, as we circled over Dover, we could see the boat waiting in the harbour below us. We had arrived considerably later than if we had plodded on by car. Moreover I had to find my way to the quay from the cliff where Merlin had "force-landed", carrying my suitcase and hobbling in my first pair of high-heeled shoes.

The bridegroom was not pleased to see me on the boat and became less so as sea-sickness took its toll of him. Jeanette's high spirits made him feel no happier; and by the time we arrived in Paris their first quarrel had reached its zenith.

By malignant chance, up to this time all the marriages at which I was a bridesmaid had ended in calamity. This one later proved to be no exception.

Jeanette took me to the address of the family chosen to polish me. Night had fallen. We stood on the pavement together, both shivering a little, for each was preparing to face a differ-ent unknown. The street-lighting illuminated the name-plates beneath the row of bells. Number four was the one we needed. Jeanette pressed the bell twice.

"Oh," she said suddenly, looking again at the nameplate, "this is not a French name."

"But it's the right name," I said. "Look, it's on my label."

"But it's not French. It's Russian."

Slowly and silently the heavy door swung open revealing a great void of darkness.

"You will not mind if I do not come up the four stair-cases?" Jeanette asked.

"Of course not," I said. After all, the bridegroom had some claim on her time on the first evening of their honeymoon.

She gave me a gentle push and I went in. Horribly, without a sound, the door shut behind me.

3

ON THE WHOLE my time in Paris was not very rewarding. I learned little French and only a few Russian habits. I came home still unpolished.

My easily won music cup had deluded my parents into a conviction that I must be musical. They sent me therefore to the Royal College of Music, where I made some good friends.

Also I learned to love London. During the first year I lugged my music-case and violin round on foot to save my bus-fares for the cinema. The next year I saved shoe-leather as well as bus-fares by living near the College.

Soon my parents realised that I should never play in the Queen's Hall and changed their tactics again. I was to be presented and go to some dances. At supper, after the curtsying in Buckingham Palace, I found a girl from school stuffing cake into her glove for her little brother, and began to enjoy it.

The dances were all very much the same, once I had passed the stage of having to hide in the ladies' cloakroom in case I was seen without a man. Chaperones, that season, had gone out. When they came in again the following season, débutantes were spared the indignity of having to make their own arrangements to be asked to dance.

Erroll was at the Royal Naval College, Greenwich, where the sub-lieutenants are encouraged to live a social life. He and his brother officers helped to make that summer unforgettably delightful. Cousins up at Oxford and Cambridge provided variations in the gaiety. At Northrepps, my cousins Joe and Hugh took me to parties.

In order to keep up with engagements, I went to Woolworth's and bought a paper-pattern and discovered how to make a dress. From then onwards Rhalou and I were able to burst out in something new whenever we wanted to. When I was not in London at parties, I worked away with the sewing-machine in the rectory schoolroom, or sat under the trees blind-hemming evening dresses for forthcoming dances.

One night my best young man said to me at the Caledonian Ball, "Why don't you do something useful? My sister makes her own garden frocks."

"Oh, I don't know," I said idly; "I'd rather dance and sing like the grasshopper."

This satisfying deception led to further concealments. I was exchanging girlish confidences with another débutante in the ladies' cloakroom at the Berkeley, when she complained,

"I don't know how Daddy expects me to manage on my dress allowance. I only get five hundred a year now my sister's come out. Where did you get that heavenly check suit?"

"Margaret Marks," I lied, and then added as an after-thought; "it was made for me."

I didn't really care whether she believed me or not; but I had no intention of revealing that our dress allowances, which included travelling expenses, never amounted to more than ten shillings a week.

But such pride lost me my best young man. He must have wanted an active girl who showed she could sew and get things done, not a grasshopper who, although she might sing for him in the summer, he might have to work for in the winter. His attentions dwindled and his letters ceased. When autumn came, the leaves shared my grief and turned a sad brown, making old masters of the landscape instead of bush fires.

I drifted gloomily into a succession of badly-paid jobs. I was a nursery-maid, a governess, a chauffeuse, a scene-shifter, a ballet dancer's dresser, and then I tried to emigrate to Canada. I enrolled as a mobile Sunday school teacher and took a course at a garage on heavy maintenance, for I would have to drive and care for a ten-hundredweight truck fitted out as a caravan and classroom. Just before we were due to sail I received a letter from the head telling me that I had been struck off the list as being too irresponsible. I was annoyed at the time, but I dare say she was right.

I applied for a job advertised in *The Times* under a box number. A young companion, preferably musical, willing to travel, was wanted.

A reply in an old-ladyish hand came, asking me to go for an interview to a South Kensington address, taking my instrument. I decided to make my instrument the piano, carrying my fiddle as a substitute. When I went off for the interview, dressed suitably in dark blue with a quiet little lace collar, I never for one moment expected not to find a dear, dotty old lady with rheumatism and enough money to spend going to Cannes in the spring.

I found the flat in a big rambling Victorian block which had carried its years badly but was still expensive. I rang the bell and an Indian in native dress let me in. Across the wide hall another Indian, with his arms folded on his chest, guarded a door. Words were exchanged between them, and the guard stepped aside, for the door, after a discreet knock, to be opened.

I was shown into a drawing-room furnished heavily with a good deal of plush and mahogany. I looked for the dotty old lady, but could see only a rather stout, white-haired Indian gentleman with one finger missing. He wore a well-cut suit of Harris tweed.

As soon as I was in the room he walked past me and locked the door, putting the key into his pocket. He waved to the piano.

"Play, please."

I sat down and played the Chopin waltz I had prepared for my dotty old lady.

"Can't you play something with a tune?" he said. "'The Blue-bells of Scotland' is nice." I played 'The Bluebells of Scotland', trying to sound as much like a musical-box as possible, and I could see he was well pleased.

"Good," he said; "now come and sit down for a talk. I want someone who can sew on my buttons and keep me proper company—not a girl who keeps running out to post letters. In fact you would have to agree never to go out without me—never. But I have many interests, cricket for instance, and crime. Have a glass of wine?"

"No, thank you," I said, looking nervously towards the locked door.

"A cigarette?"

"I don't smoke," not even undoped cigarettes, I felt like adding.

"I must insist on your drinking my health. Here, read the paper while I pour out your wine."

He handed me a copy of the *News of the World* in which every connection with crime had been marked with a red cross. I felt a wild desire to rush to the locked door and batter on it.

"If I find I like you," I heard behind me, "then I take you back to India and you have many horses to ride and cars to drive— Rolls Royces only. But you must not want to come back. That would not be fair to me."

It was not the horses and the Rolls Royces that made me say what I did, but an extraordinary trait in my character, which always makes me do everything in my power to land any job I apply for, however unsuitable I am for it, or it for me. Perhaps the many jobs I had already lost had some bearing on it, or possibly it is merely a simple inability to say no to anything. "I'll do it," I said.

"Then you will be paid thirty shillings a week," I was told. "Not that you will need even that, as you will be resident, of course. But it will prove that you are mine."

"When do I start?"

"Now."

"But my clothes?" I said, playing for time. "I must fetch my luggage."

"We will go out together and buy some new."

I saw a vision of myself going into a fitting-room at Harrods to try on some undergarment, while he stood outside firmly holding on to my outer clothes against my escape. I should be forced to climb over the top into the next fitting-room, and perhaps surprise some other half-dressed lady as I dashed to the security of the manager's office. I should probably be locked up, but eventually I should get away.

"We will go together now to your room."

My new employer called to his servant, and then went to the door to unlock it.

"I don't want the job!" I cried, almost hysterically, as though pleading for mercy.

"You don't?" the old Indian sounded disappointed.

"No."

"Are you sure?"

"Yes yes, I'm sure."

"What a pity," he sighed. "It is so difficult to find a nice girl who would suit me. I shall have to go without my buttons. Thank you for coming." He held out his four-fingered hand, and I forced myself to shake it. The brown skin was soft and dry.

"Good-bye," I said.

But how ridiculous! I thought when I was out on the pavement. My imagination had worked me up into a fine old frenzy that time. Obviously he was just a harmless lonely old man who wanted young companionship, without having yet mastered the customs of this country. There must be many a dotty old lady in South Kensington afraid to let her paid companion post a letter in case she left her for ever. I almost felt like going back and reaccepting the job, to show I believed in the old man, almost, but not quite.

That evening at a dinner party I told the story against myself, expecting at any rate a laugh or two. But the story was received with grave shakings of heads as though I was too young to know what I was talking about. Afterwards the wife of the Lord Chancellor asked me to give her the Indian's address.

"Is it the horses or the Rolls Royces?" I teased her.

A few days later Lucy, with whom I shared a flat, opened the door to a stranger.

"He says he's from Scotland Yard," Lucy came and told me with a doubting giggle, "and he'd like you to go along with him."

"Don't be silly," I said. "Who is he?"

"Honestly," Lucy assured me. "Go and see for yourself."

I thought of all the mistakes I might have made lately—driving offences, unstamped insurance cards, getting pennies back from telephone-boxes by pressing button B.

But I could think of none that would interest Scotland Yard. It was not until I was in the police car that I understood the reason for the police wanting me. They wished to discuss the South Kensington Indian's companionship.

At the entrance to the famous "Yard," a uniformed policeman nodded to us to pass up a long flight of stairs.

I was led through a broad passage to a bare office overlooking the river, where I was told to wait.

Soon I was joined by another plain-clothes man, who began to question me in the voice that one assumes for playing the parlour game of Murder.

I answered every question with a definite bias in favour of my near-employer. A lot of fuss, I implied, was being made about nothing.

"I'm quite sure he's a perfectly harmless old gentleman."

"That," said the inspector slowly, "is exactly what we feared. If he can make you, a sensible young lady, feel quite safe in his presence, there is no end to the trouble he can create."

"Oh, but I didn't really feel *safe* in his presence," I said quickly.

"No? Then why do you take his side now?"

"Because I think he's been misunderstood. I wish I'd never mentioned him to anyone."

"Young lady," said the inspector patiently, "if only more people would talk about such things, it would be a much poorer look-out for criminals."

"Criminals?"

"You may be surprised to hear that we have been watching a gentleman of your description for some years. He has a way of coming in and out of the country without a passport."

"How does he do that?"

"Day trips across the Channel from the south-coast resorts. There and back in a day, no passport needed. They'll have to be stopped. Too many criminals get away like that." I longed to hear more. "In the past, at times corresponding with the mysterious disappearances of our dark friend, a number of young ladies—soft-hearted young ladies like yourself—have been reported missing." The picture loomed up of the soft-hearted sensible young ladies like myself lounging about in the harem in yashmaks. They all had the faces of hospital nurses.

"It's not exactly *white slave traffic*, is it?" I asked, fascinated.

"We haven't proved anything yet."

"But we could!" I said with sudden excitement, changing sides without more ado. "I could go back and take the job after all. Even if I'm not allowed out to post a letter, I could make myself easy for you to have watched, at any rate till we got to Eastbourne pier. By then I could probably manage to slip you all the information you wanted. I don't quite know how, but I'd find a way—hidden in refuse, perhaps, which your men could pick up in the dustbins."

The inspector smiled.

"It's very good of you to suggest it," he said, "but it wouldn't do, you know."

"I'd be quite safe, honestly," I insisted.

"As a matter of fact the gentleman you met has already gone from the address where you were interviewed."

"Where is he now?"

"I wish I knew. I asked you to come and see me, thinking, before I had the pleasure of meeting you of course, that you might be able to throw some light on the matter."

"Alas, no light," I said sadly.

That was the end of that job.

Disheartened, I returned to the rectory to help my mother to encourage Rhalou to take an interest in the elaborate trousseau which was being made for her. Rhalou was going to be married in a month's time. She was beautiful, slim and charming, but quite unable to apply herself to anything so worldly as dress. Clothed for comfort in a kind of a square Greek tunic, she sat with her farrowing sow, while my mother and I stood by trying to wring some preference out of her for pleats or gathers.

On the morning of the wedding, when her eight bridesmaids were already dressed, she was still down in the paddock picking stones out of her pony's feet. Her hair, which had been set the day before to give it time to settle, hung round her face in damp ringlets, caused by the dew rising above the mattress on which she had slept out on the lawn, with her two Skye terriers at her feet. Among the bridesmaids were Lucy, who had arrived the night before from London, and Lorema, who had come straight from school. Rhalou had not bothered to prevent pale blue taffeta dresses with bunches of fawn roses on them from being chosen for the bridesmaids by the dressmaker. Holding these up out of the mud, Lucy and Lorema hurried down to the paddock to finish the pony's feet, while Rhalou started back to the house to change into her wedding dress. On her way, she was unable to resist mucking out the ferrets.

A window at the back of the house shot open and my mother leaned out to call, through force of habit.

"Rhalou! If you don't come in at once we shall go without you."

Somehow we managed to knock Rhalou's hair back into shape. She crammed on the tiara of jewelled orange blossom which had belonged to our great-grandmother, then she stepped into her wedding dress and pulled it up.

I clipped the train on to her shoulders. Lucy handed her a sheaf of lilies; and my mother threw her Honiton lace heirloom over the lot, rather as though she were applying a dust-sheet to the drawing-room sofa before spring-cleaning.

Yet, as Rhalou came into church on my father's arm, she looked so touchingly lovely that even her tough old hunting cronies wept with delight.

The familiar musty smell floated up from the ancient oak pews. As children we had pressed our noses to the book-rests of those pews while we knelt on lumpy hassocks, out of which flew an occasional moth.

"Rhalou," I could hear our bishop cousin saying, as though he were asking her to pass the toast at breakfast, "will you take this man to be your lawful wedded husband?"

The reception for the five hundred guests was held in the newly restored medieval castle, which lay in all its beauty in the valley below the church. This hospitality was a wedding present from the owner of the castle.

Afterwards a bridesmaids' dance was held at our old school. In the prefects' study, outside the stationery cupboard, and in the place where the hockey balls were painted, three young men asked me to marry them. Two took it for granted I would never dream of marrying anyone else, and the third obviously asked me only because he could no longer hope to get the right answer from Rhalou.

When Lucy and Lorema and I had written the last of Rhalou's thank-you letters, had helped to clear up the debris, and had packed off Rhalou's animals in a horsebox to her new home, Lorema returned to school and Lucy went to South Africa. And I went to London and got myself a job illustrating toffee-papers.

4

IN A STUDIO FLAT over a bird-fancier's, I lived with three somewhat Bohemian friends. Except for my toffee-papers, which even at the height of the toffee season could only be looked upon as stepping-stones to a living wage, we were all out of work of one kind or another.

One Saturday evening, fired by my artistic success, I decided to experiment with something bigger. On a tile of linoleum that had come out of the kitchen floor, I began making my first lino-cut. While the others played any-number-a-side ping-pong with whoever happened to drop in, I sat at a side table intent on art.

Among those who dropped in was my cousin Montagu, who always kept a fatherly eye on me when I was in London. He was on his way home from some smart function, and with him was an old friend who had been to the same party. The ping-pong became five-a-side. I went on with the lino-cut.

Presently my design of a girl ski-ing began to spring unexpectedly into shape. Then I noticed that Montagu's friend was sitting silently beside me, trimming away the surplus linoleum, an eyeglass fixed into his right eye. Neither of us spoke, but I could not help noticing the colour of his hair, a colour associated with early autumn trees. There was nothing else of the country about him. His hands were smooth and his clothes cut with military precision. Out of consideration for the bird-fancier below, he had been playing ping-pong in his socks. They were nice socks, quiet yet at the same time distinguished.

My chisel slipped and I cut my finger. Montagu's friend whipped a monogrammed silk handkerchief out of his pocket and wrapped it tenderly round my finger. Without having yet exchanged a word, we both fell in love.

Montagu came and sat by us. "Don't believe a word he says," he said of his friend. Then he took him away.

The next day the King abdicated. It was cold and foggy anyway, but the news added to the gloom in the streets, where Londoners' steps moved heavily with unhappiness. But my heart sang, and for the moment that was enough. Fate would throw us together again, I knew.

But fate was not pressed hard. Montagu's friend himself wrote me a formal note asking me to have tea with him at his club. The fact that I could not accept for a few days was of no consequence. We had a lifetime before us.

His club was in Piccadilly, looking over Green Park. We sat in a beautifully proportioned room drinking tea and talking politely. He offered to help me find a new job, for the toffee-papers had slipped away during the Abdication. I wanted to offer to sew on a shirt button that I noticed was loose; but it seemed too forward.

Our next meeting had more of the element of chance in it. Both of us had the same idea of seeing Montagu off from Victoria to winter sports. Montagu waved his ski-boots out of the train window to us. His friend took me out to dinner.

Montagu returned a fortnight later and faced us both in the club. He was deeply concerned.

"I don't know how I'll explain this to your mother," he said unhappily. "It's true I thought you might find something in common, but I never dreamed you'd want to marry each other."

Donald and I both laughed delightedly.

When we were alone, we talked of the home we should have and the children, and how we would spend our life together. Under this enchantment we were oblivious of such essentials as an adequate and steady income. A new play Donald had just finished would see to all that.

The play did not.

With the gradual realisation that the play which he had been writing for five years could not succeed, Donald's conscience began to nag him.

My father increased his sense of guilt by reminding him that I was only twenty-one and he considerably older. "You're spoiling her chances," my father said, with, I suspect, a particular suitor in mind—short, dull, rich, and consciously successful.

As a matter of course, the rest of the family put the idea of any prospective spouse through their own particular form of grilling, which only true love could survive. Every small fault was dragged out and held up to the light at breakfast, lunch, and tea; and every possible source of incompatibility was vastly exaggerated. There was something to be said for this rather ruthless method of making sure that we knew our own minds.

I was cured of one young man—mercifully, I now see— by my sisters' constant reminders of the flatness of the top of his head, which was easy to indicate by drawing a square box. This horrid symbol would appear on the telephone pad while I talked to him, on the wet sand when we went bathing, or on a breathed-on glass when we were drinking. Nothing was said, but steadily my sisters wore me down. I became sickened by the sight of that box-like head.

Since there was nothing to be found against Donald except his age and lack of riches, I was put to the test by cuttings pinned to my pillow about bearded old-age pensioners marrying barmaids.

When Donald started too, I became furious.

"I'm spoiling your chances," he repeated.

Only Norrie said: "He's too good for you."

Perhaps, after all, he wanted to marry somebody else! With this grim thought I left the job I had just got, and went to Land's End with Lucy.

One of Lucy's outstanding qualities is her ability to make even a trip down a coal-mine into a holiday fraught with beauty. A month with Lucy on a Cornish farm, even if it could not cure me of Donald, brought about a sense of tranquillity that was useful.

Lucy took me to Skye, to a romantic cliff-edge castle where her father had taken a grouse-moor with deerstalking and sea-fishing. It belonged to a young laird with fiery whiskers and hairy plus-fours to match. We gazed at him reverently in kirk on the Sabbath. In the evenings the guests were so imbued with simple happiness from days on the hill or the loch or the sea, that our parlour games took their tone from it. Even important political guests and their mature wives displayed themselves in charades as the local postmistress, or, rising from an inverted umbrella in pink undies and loosened hair, portrayed Venus hatching from her scallop shell.

Sometimes I escaped from the mass activities of the house party, and wrote poetry while Lucy sketched. The poetry was partly illegible and did not scan; but Arbuthnot, Lucy's brother, would oblige me by trying to read it.

> The hills, purple-covered and brown with half-turned bracken,
> Reflecting and becoming one with the loch,
> And so achieving undulating feet and—gravy—

"Are you sure it's gravy, V?" he asked, puzzled.

Pulling lobster-pots up into a boat, Lucy and Arbuthnot and I discussed abstract love and each other, in the third person.

"It must be a great handicap to Arbuthnot, his hyper-sensitivity," I said thoughtfully.

"I don't think it is," Lucy said. "He's always been like that. I don't suppose he notices it."

"Poor V! Can't help noticing hers," said Arbuthnot. "Damn! The bait's gone."

"Though really V's greatest handicap," said Lucy, withdrawing a crab from the wicker pot, "is being so hyperbolical."

"Dear V!" said Arbuthnot. "Never mind. She's looking more tranquil, don't you think, Lucy?"

"Yes, much. You can always tell with V."

They treated me like a bruised flower. After the love thera-peutics of my own brothers and sisters, Lucy's and Arbuthnot's were like balm.

The fellow guest at the tiller—so young that she had not even yet begun reading the *New Statesman*—told me years later that the snatches of conversation that blew her way gave her an impression that it must all be on a very high intellectual level. Perhaps we too believed it was.

I returned to London to yet another job, believing myself cured; but somehow it was a strange relief to find that I was not. At one of those giant Foyle's luncheons I could see Donald in the distance talking to one of the speakers. And so it was bound to happen, as long as we continued to live in the same city. I would see his back as he moved away into a crowd, hear his voice, recognise his handwriting. We had too many inter-ests in common for me to be able to avoid him altogether, as I vowed I would. Sometimes it was not his back, not his voice, not his handwriting, but somebody else's like enough to his that I noticed, and my heart turned over just the same.

* * * * *

Rhalou was beginning to have babies. Eventually she had six. Merlin and Erroll were married too, and filling cradles when they were not at sea. I love all babies, just as some people love all dogs. Only four dogs in my life have ever crept into my heart; but whenever I see a baby, however hideous, however dirty, however spotty, some gland gets working in me and I want to adopt it. I loved all my little nephews as passionately as any other babies, perhaps rather more so, and became an office bore about them.

I liked my job, and for the first time in my life worked hard because I wanted to. When my annual holiday fell due I knew I should enjoy it more than any holiday before because it was, without a doubt, the best earned. Besides, I had planned to meet Lucy and Arbuthnot in Brittany, and my soul was ripe for more of their soothing influence after a year in London trying to avoid Donald.

On the last day of August—it was 1939—I boarded a steamer for St. Malo. War rumours were strengthening and I seemed to be the only passenger on board: for the desire of most English tourists was already to leave the continent, not to go there.

From the train I could see men and horses gathering in groups in the market places of every town we passed. But, apart from being kissed in a tunnel by an over-patriotic chef who was already celebrating a French victory, my journey was uneventful.

Lucy met me at Concarneau and drove me to the tiny white-painted, sea-washed hotel on the pink rocks of the west coast. Arbuthnot was waving from the flat roof, wearing shorts of the same russet sail-cloth that I could see stretched above the fishing-boats out to sea. Lucy had bought a pair for me too, and a pair for herself. There was something touching about this gesture which reminded me of the comforts of the nursery, where gaiters and leggings were all alike. It made me feel wanted, and was more than equal to a discussion in the third person.

So were bathing in clear sea-pools, and the delicious French food and wine, and dancing in the little bar of the hotel till the buckle of my shoe fell off. By now the holiday was made all the sweeter because we knew that at any hour it might be snatched away from us.

The morning after I arrived, Lucy and I joined Arbuthnot for coffee and rolls. As we went into his room he flicked a telegram across his bed. I knew before reading it that it meant we must go home. RETURN AT ONCE COMMANDING OFFICER.

"I suppose our commanding officers in the F.A.N.Y.s will send ours later," said Lucy; and this, at the time, seemed to us a most ridiculous joke. The F.A.N.Y. meetings we had attended from time to time during the past year had mostly taken the form of sherry parties. But before we left the hotel our telegrams arrived, commanding us to join our units, but omitting to say where they were.

Grudgingly I packed again the things I had only just unpacked. The hotelier, wearing riding-breeches smelling of moth-balls, for he had been recalled as a remount officer, waved us away.

"Come back after the war," he called.

We drove off to St. Malo, expecting every time we stopped for food or petrol to hear that war had been declared. But somehow here, rolling along the French roads between the poplars, it was difficult to take the war seriously, with only our three selves to offer opinions about the international situation.

At St. Malo we found long queues of English people waiting to return to Southampton. We soon learned there was no hope of leaving that day. We went round the hotels trying to find beds for the night, but without success; so we ate what we felt might be our last square meal, and then dragged such warm clothes as we had with us out of the car and picked our way over the rocks in the dark to sleep on the sand.

It was a beautiful night and little waves rippled in not far below our feet; but now it was impossible not to feel fully conscious of the fact that the fate of Europe—and perhaps of the world—was hanging by a thread which must surely break.

Late into the night we three talked, lying on our stomachs and tracing patterns with our fingers in the invisible sand, probing into our pasts in search of prophetic patterns, even more impossible to see in our short lives. With the breaking of dawn we became frivolous and then fell deeply asleep.

When we woke and stood up to shake the sand out of our clothes and hair, we knew that war was serious and already standing over us like a drooping canopy.

By abandoning the car, we were able to crush ourselves aboard a small boat intended for several hundred fewer passengers than it carried. The crossing took all day, but the sun shone warmly and we were able to find a small space on the deck where we could make a small camp for ourselves and read T. S. Eliot out loud to each other.

At Southampton the prospect of war seemed much more real than in France. Arbuthnot, because of the genuine urgency of his recall, was the first off the boat. He turned to wave from the gangway. Something about the solemnity of his gesture brought home, more deeply than any of our talk the night before, what war might mean for our generation.

Lucy and I sat down on the deck again, with Arbuthnot's watch, which he had left with us to be mended, swinging on its chain from my hand. The crowds pressed off the boat by the gangways.

"John and Merlin and Erroll too," said Lucy out loud, thinking of our brothers in the Navy.

"And Alec and Dick and Dear Steaming Kettle," I said, thinking of friends we had grown up with.

"And Thomas and John E. and all those battalions of cousins of yours," said Lucy.

"Yes," I said, "I suppose they'll all be old enough." I got up to put Arbuthnot's watch safely into Lucy's bag. "Oh, they'll come back," I said impatiently.

Some of them did.

It was the last time I saw Arbuthnot until after the war. He was wounded in Malaya and led an escape party from the hospital in Singapore when it fell. He was given the Military Cross. In a small open boat, with thirty men on board, he rigged up a sail and captained them to safety.

"What about Donald and Norrie?" Lucy asked suddenly. "Will they go?"

"Yes, I'm sure they will. They were hurt by the last war; but it's still the biggest thing of their lives—judging by their talk. It gave them something—I don't know what it was—that they haven't been able to find again since."

In the first war Donald and Norrie had both joined up, under-age, from school. The war left Donald with a damaged lung and Norrie with only one leg.

"Of course," I went on, "they're not fit enough or young enough to go into the forefront of the battle; though they wouldn't thank you for telling them so. They'll manage to get in somehow."

Lucy chuckled.

"It looks like their lot to have to diddle their ages to get into a war," she said.

Lucy and I were the last off the boat. We telephoned our mothers to tell them we were in England, and then almost fell with exhaustion into the nearest hotel wagon, without realising it would take us to the biggest and most expensive hotel in Southampton. We were too tired to care, and booked a room on the top floor, expecting to fall asleep at once under the luxurious pink silk eiderdowns on the beds. But the sound of the plodding feet of a sentry on the roof created a much greater sense of suspense than even the headlines of the English papers could do. Every moan and bleat from the ships' sirens down in the docks seemed to be going to work itself up into the wail of an air-raid siren announcing that the enemy were on their way without a formal declaration of war.

We went down to breakfast, ready to start taking the F.A.N.Y.s seriously after all.

"Once the war starts I want to be in it," I said, "up to the hilt."

"Anybody'd think you'd been in the last one," Lucy grinned. "You talk like Donald and Norrie."

"Well, you know I can't bear being left out of a party," I reminded her. "Besides," I added more honestly, "I think it'll be less frightening to do something about it."

Suddenly we looked up to see Norrie standing beside us.

As soon as he heard from my mother that we were here, he got into his car and drove along the coast to take us home, out of harm's way.

"But Verily wants to stay in harm's way," Lucy told him. "She thinks it's safer."

Back at the rectory I found Erroll on leave, champing for a ship. He and Lorema and I picked and ate unripe figs, and romped on the lawn till the lengthening shadows reached us. This was not at all the spirit in which I had expected to meet a war. It was like an ordinary evening in the summer holidays. Will this patch of grass be here when the war's over? I wondered as I got up to go in for supper.

Next day the F.A.N.Y.s sent me a uniform and a message to say I was wanted at once in London. Erroll drove me to the station.

"Here's me," he said, "been in the service since I was thirteen, and along comes a war and you're in it in half an hour, leaving me at home in my old grey flannels and nothing to do."

"You never know," I called out of the train window. "There may still not be a war."

A few weeks later Erroll was chasing U-Boats in the North Sea in a submarine.

At the F.A.N.Y. depot in London I was directed somewhat vaguely with several other girls, as self-conscious in their uniform as I was, to the Ford works at Dagenham to drive cars "off the lines" to Aldershot—presumably till they ceased to come off the lines. We were told we should have to find our own billets for the next few days.

About half a dozen of us straggled off to Dagenham and waited for half the day beside the cool river. Only three cars were handed over to us to drive to Aldershot. With a burst of zeal, most of the F.A.N.Y.s piled themselves into the cars when they learned that no more would be ready for delivery that day. A pretty, amused-looking girl and I decided to conserve our strength and go back to London. We could think of no useful purpose we could serve in the back of a car going to Aldershot. Elizabeth had no uniform yet: her only equipment was an unstuffed palliasse, which she hoped to fill with straw and sleep on when the war started.

I went straight to Hampstead and billeted myself with old friends of Donald's, Phyl and her little girl Portia. Portia hugged me round the knees and tried on my greatcoat and gas-mask.

Next day at Dagenham there were three times as many cars to be delivered as there were F.A.N.Y.s to drive them: so we shuttled backwards and forwards for hours till they had all been handed over at Aldershot.

When I got back to London in the evening there was such a feeling of urgency in the air that you could almost see it. Even the cosy, silvery barrage-balloons looked belligerent. Women in uniform were still a rarity; and I found my khaki being regarded with the same silent shaking of the head as tanks and guns received when they rattled through the streets. But to some it was more than just a sign of the times. I was stood up for in buses; and when I went into a café an elderly woman insisted on paying for my snack. In Piccadilly Circus a dear old flower-girl pushed two bunches of violets into my arms.

"Tike 'em, ducks, wiv my luv. It's good to see a young girl do her dooty." I thought with shame of my skimped duty at Dagenham the day before. But I knew what she meant. It was just the general idea of everybody being in it that touched her heart, even the young girls.

From Phyl's snug little house in old Hampstead you could look down over London. When I got there at dusk we went up to the top room to look at the barrage-balloons. We had never seen so many up together before.

"It'll be war tomorrow," we said, "for sure."

During the night such a violent thunderstorm broke out that I shivered in my bed.

"Or could it be Hitler's secret weapon?" I suggested to Phyl.

"Or God's wrath?" said Phyl.

A zig-zag of lightning gashed the sky, splashing the room in light.

"Bet you fourpence the barrage-balloons get struck," I said.

Sunday morning dawned bright and clear.

"Fourpence!" I said, looking out of the window. "Not a balloon in sight. The whole lot have been struck."

At eleven o'clock the Prime Minister announced over the radio that we had declared war on Germany. Dramatically, less than two minutes later, the first war-time air-raid sirens sounded over London. Phyl and Portia and I left the radio to tear upstairs to the top window to see what would happen.

"Below us lies London in all her summer greenery," I observed.

"But how long before she lies lower?" asked Phyl.

"Give back your fourpence!" Portia suddenly squealed.

From all over London, from the green of the squares, the gardens, and the parks, silver barrage-balloons shining in the morning sun were floating silently up into the sky.

"If this is the war," I said, "it's much prettier than I expected."

"It is the war," Portia said. "The Prime Minister said so."

Soon the all-clear sounded. The alarm had been false. It was only the Duke of Windsor flying in. He wanted to be there at the start.

5

THERE WAS NOT much about the beginning of the war that tallied with my notions of what war would be like. Rationing, which I imagined would be clamped down on us on Monday morning, was still a long way off. A few delicacies ceased to be imported or manufactured. And quite early in the war I bought my last packet of banana-cream biscuits. But it was a year before I ate my last banana.

My plans for concealing my fears under a dashing adventurous life came to nothing. For one thing, now that war had been declared, there was nothing for the moment to fear. Eagerly I volunteered to be sent abroad; but when the time came to be posted from London I found myself instead back in Sussex in a house I knew well, with about thirty other F.A.N.Y.s, including Elizabeth with her unstuffed palliasse.

We were commanded by a bubbly-haired old actress who, as the niece of a senior army officer, took her position very seriously. In her talk she mingled a certain amount of army jargon, picked up at her uncle's breakfast table, with the normal chatter we understood of hats and actors and horses. Sometimes, judging by her modes of addressing us, she saw us as Mayfair Débutantes and sometimes as Men Going Over The Top.

The idea behind our camping in this big and beautiful house was that we should be able to drive ambulances for the army. At first we had no ambulances, and hung about wistfully wishing we had. Then we were allotted an assortment of commandeered furniture-vans, fish-carts, and carriers.

Within a week of our collecting them, I had the misfortune to be the first F.A.N.Y. to crash one into a gatepost.

The C.O. came running out to look at the damage. Several army expressions must have floated up from her subconscious, but for the moment all she could say was a reproving,

"Really, Bruce, it's too tiresome!"

She went back to her office, which she called The Orderly Room, and must have sat down to think hard of something with more of a military tang.

A few minutes later, while I was getting ready for lunch, two F.A.N.Y.s of the quiet, useful, obedient type came into the bedroom which I shared with four others (including one whose claim to fame was that her husband had been fallen on by Queen Mary in her recent motor accident). The two F.A.N.Y.s stood in a waiting attitude, one each side of me.

"Want to borrow a comb?" I asked affably.

"You're under arrest," said one.

"I'm what?" I asked.

"Under arrest. We've had orders to close in on you and march you to the orderly room without your cap or belt."

I giggled. This was just the sort of joke Elizabeth and I had with each other, but it was funnier coming from these two.

"Oh," said one to the other, "she can't. The C.O. never thought of that. Our belts are stitched on to our tunics."

"Then, without your cap, fall in!" said the other.

"I say, are you serious?" I asked with some surprise, now remembering the episode of the fallen gate-post.

"C.O.'s orders. Quick march."

I put on my tunic and, still buttoning it, trotted merrily along between them, hoping to meet Elizabeth on the way downstairs. But Elizabeth was not about. To my amazement, everybody we passed turned away as though in shame. I had knocked a good many gate-posts down in my time, but nobody had ever before felt so deeply about it as this.

In the orderly room I had an idea which I felt might interest our dramatic C.O. I saluted her.

"You can't salute without a cap on," she remembered, and then gave various conflicting orders to my escorts.

"The Prisoner To Be Confined In A Cell," she ended up and I was marched away to the green dressing-room which I had known as such since I was a child. I sat down on the bed waiting to see what would happen next. I could hear my escorts moving about outside as they guarded me.

Soon one of them brought my lunch on a tray. Her eyes were downcast and the tray shook a little. After all that ceremonial, I expected dry bread and water, which is what we were given as children when we were sent to bed in disgrace. I was quite surprised to be allowed ordinary sausages and mash, which was followed by apple tart brought by the other escort.

To my intense delight, secreted in the apple tart was a slip of paper on which dear Elizabeth had written, *"Keep a stiff upper lip for the honour of the Third."* I was glad her eyes were not downcast.

A few minutes later I heard weeping outside, followed by muffled footsteps.

The gardener's wife came in to take my tray away. She handed me a box of chocolates.

"I dunno, I'm sure," she said. "One of the young ladies give me this to give you. The one outside was crying her eyes out and saying she couldn't go on. And half of them downstairs wouldn't touch their lunch. You'd think there'd been a murder. Three left the table sudden-like, and that pretty young Lady Victoria burst into tears and ran upstairs in a dreadful state."

"But what's it all about?" I asked. "What's happened?"

"Haven't they told you?"

"No."

"You're going to be court-martialled."

"Oh, dear!" I said. "Then I'd better clean my buttons."

My next visitor was the M.T. sergeant, a tough-looking lady who was rarely seen out of oily overalls.

"Please tell me," I asked her anxiously, "did I kill somebody?"

"Who? You? Not that I know of."

"Then what's this all about?"

"You've done something serious, my gal," she said, taking her cigarette out of the corner of her mouth. "You've damaged government property."

"But this place belongs to my father's churchwarden."

"As far as we're concerned, it's government property. What I want to know is, would you prefer to be tried by men or women?"

"Men," I said, "every time."

"I think the C.O. would prefer to keep this to ourselves. So I'll tell her you'd rather have women. I shall be on your side, of course."

This was something new. So far the sergeant had never found herself able to be on my side.

"I'm the prisoner's friend," she said, smoothing down her Eton crop and wiping her hand on the seat of her overalls.

"Oh," I said. "Who'll be my enemy?"

"The president of the court. That's the C.O. Rather fun, eh?" She rollocked out of the room.

As my guard had mutinied, it was the M.T. sergeant who escorted me down to what used to be, before the arrival of the F.A.N.Y.s, the small drawing-room. The C.O. had herself chosen a jury and three witnesses, who had been nowhere near the gate-post at the time of the impact.

I thought of Elizabeth's message and tried to see how funny it all was. But the jury and the witnesses were all so painfully embarrassed that I began to feel as though I was having my appendix out in a public waiting-room. The only person who appeared to be enjoying herself was the prisoner's friend. She seized the opportunity of making hay with her senior officer, whom I found myself feeling quite sorry for. After all, the C.O. had obviously set out to do what she felt was her duty to the country.

Two greyhounds wandered in and, rather as though they had come into church, were hustled discreetly out.

My mind wandered off on to other things while the president and the prisoner's friend became more and more irrelevant, only occasionally attracting the unwilling attention of the jury.

I was surprised out of my reverie by the pronouncement,

"Not guilty."

"But surely—" I started to object, then thought better of it. If the gate-post had been proved still intact, let it rest at that. I was dismissed.

The tension was broken. I was surrounded by F.A.N.Y.s, jury and otherwise, shaking my hand and congratulating me as though I had shot the winning goal in a school match. One of the dormitories instantly gave a feast for me, delving under their beds to produce drinks and cakes and fruit. The C.O., delving back again into her subconscious for an appropriate term, brought out a beauty.

"If you'd been found guilty, there would of course have been The Question Of Mitigation Of Sentence."

* * * * *

A few weeks later our assorted civilian vehicles were exchanged for genuine army ambulances, which we scrubbed inside and out with our own nail-brushes. In a day or two we packed ourselves into them and drove off to a sea-port to establish an ambulance base in a requisitioned children's home.

Elizabeth and I were given beds in the boys' dormitory which, except for the slight inappropriateness of the adjoining sanitary arrangements, was comfortable enough.

Our job was to collect stretcher-cases from the hospital-ships docking by the quay below. But, apart from men who had broken their legs playing football, or had eaten too much French food, we had few patients.

One evening, with Elizabeth as co-driver, I was detailed to form part of a convoy to a big hospital seventy miles away. It was already dusk when we bumped over the railway lines on the quay and came to a standstill not many feet from the water's edge. The white hospital-ship looked small and defenceless as it slid quietly into the harbour. Most of the stretcher-cases were carried straight into the waiting hospital-train. Five walking cases were shut into the back of my ambulance. I was not given an orderly, as I had a co-driver. All my cases were suffering from shell-shock.

It was soon dark; and the normal strain of driving in the black-out was intensified by our not knowing just how shell-shocked our patients were. We soon lost touch with the rest of the convoy.

For the first half of the journey our patients were almost eerily quiet. Then quite suddenly they began to knock on the dividing panel.

"Drive faster," said Elizabeth. I did, nearly taking a wheel off a farm cart, but getting no nearer to our convoy.

"Anyway they can't get out," I said thankfully.

"Unless they knock down the partition between us," said Elizabeth.

The patients started to hammer even more loudly.

"D'you know," said Elizabeth suddenly, "I think we ought to stop. I've had an idea."

I stopped and we went round to the back of the ambulance together and very carefully opened the door.

"Thank you, miss," said a voice. "We shan't be long. We thought you couldn't hear us."

Elizabeth and I went back to the driver's cabin, still not sure whether we had merely taken nature into consideration, or whether we had allowed five dangerous lunatics to escape.

Suddenly in the darkness I felt a horny hand on mine. For a moment I felt that, if there was any escaping to be done, it should be done by us.

"Like a cigarette, miss?" a comforting voice said.

"Oh, thank you," I said gratefully, fumbling for one, although I never smoked.

"They're all in the back now, when you want to go on."

"Then we'll shut the back doors," I said, climbing down, losing my footing, and falling into the raving lunatic's helpful arms.

We shut them in and continued the journey. All went well till after we had handed over the right number of patients to the hospital in exchange for a receipt.

Then Elizabeth suggested filling up with petrol. The ambulance carried four two-gallon cans. Elizabeth pulled one out, unscrewed it, and poured the contents into the petrol tank.

We started off down the hospital drive to join the rest of the convoy. After twenty yards the engine spluttered and died.

"I've had another idea," said Elizabeth. "It might have been water."

We got out and examined the empty can by the dim light of the hooded headlamps. WATER was painted only too boldly across it.

We spent the night in a Nissen hut, lying on three army "biscuits". It was cold and the biscuits were hard and we felt that nobody loved us.

"Never mind," said Elizabeth next morning as we sped along in the autumn sunshine, stopping for cups of coffee and cakes when we felt like it. "It was worth it."

Elizabeth and I were on night guard on Christmas night. This entailed patrolling round the vehicles for fifteen minutes every hour to see that neither they nor their petrol had been stolen. We had free access to the kitchen in between inspections and could, or anyway did, help ourselves to eggs and bacon at irregular intervals. Elizabeth had bought her fiancé a cigarette-lighter for Christmas, so our first action was to dip the sleeve of an old shirt into the petrol tank of one of the ambulances, intending to squeeze it into the lighter. But the sleeve disappeared irretrievably into the tank, and we had to resort to the somewhat meaner method of pumping the petrol out with a tyre-pump.

We spent the rest of the night decorating the holiday home with cotton wool and coloured paper, and hanging stockings up by the beds of our favourite F.A.N.Y.s.

On Boxing Day we were both posted north. Elizabeth hurried off, when we reached London, on forty-eight hours' leave to meet her fiancé for the first time since the war began. I sauntered into a telephone-box to ring up Montagu. I was not travelling north till the evening.

Somehow I never did telephone Montagu. Instead, the number dialled must have been Donald's. Oh well, I thought quickly when I heard his voice, it was Christmas time, the time of good will to all men, and soon I should be safely out of London.

Donald sounded pleased to hear from me.

"Not married yet?" he asked.

"Of course not."

"Can't you come and have lunch with me at the club and tell me all the news?"

I can't because, I thought, if I do . . .

"Yes, I'd love to," I said.

I was surprised to find he was not in uniform. To his intense disappointment he had not been found fit for combatant duties. He had refused carpet-soldier jobs offered to him at the War Office, preferring to accept an obviously civilian job at the Ministry of Information, while still hoping to get into action some other way.

We exchanged news of our friends, and then parted after a fierce quarrel of the kind usual only between close relatives. Although I seethed with anger against Donald all the way in the cold train going north, such a quarrel had something heartening about it. "Now I know I never want to see him again," is what I thought it meant.

My new depot was to me a terrible place. The F.A.N.Y.s there were more efficient and knew the rules better and so took themselves even more seriously than their southern sisters. Part of the efficiency consisted in making newcomers like myself wash all the cars. With icy rags dipped in water, which froze in the bucket, we tried to scrape frost off forty windscreens. After a few days the newcomers were moved on to clean up an army hut on a gun-site on the wind-seared marshes. I felt colder than ever and slightly ill. It was quite a relief to wake up one morning with the close red rash of German measles. A couple of days in bed with a kindly F.A.N.Y. offering to nurse me would be a welcome rest. But the military officials there knew the rules too.

I was infectious and must therefore be removed to the nearest fever hospital.

I was not very ill, but the first day of German measles can make you feel it. I had a bad headache and a high temperature, and found no joy in sitting on the floor of an empty furniture-van for a long, draughty drive through deep snow.

The fever hospital must have been designed by a southerner on one of the few summer days that this part of England could ever hope to have. The glass cubicles were joined by an open veranda leading to the only completely closed-in part, which was occupied by the sister.

The soldier-driver who handed me over patted my arm.

"Coo, chum, I don't envy you," he said.

A sullen young nurse gripped my elbow and led me into the end cubicle. It had three outside walls, made almost entirely of glass. There was no heating. A bed like a mortuary slab was made up with coarse, yellow twill sheets. Yet even that bed was attractive to me.

The nurse took my temperature while I stood, and whistled with satisfaction when she read the thermometer.

"But it's only German measles," I said.

"You're not here to diagnose your own disease," she said sharply. "Come this way please."

She led me along the snow-strewn veranda again and into a squalid bathroom. She ran a tepid bath and told me to undress and get into it. Then she took a nail-brush and scrubbed my inflamed and tickling rash with carbolic soap.

"Is this a good idea?" I asked doubtfully.

"Good idea or bad, it's routine."

One end of the bath was slightly warmer than the other. I crouched there thinking how angry I should be if only I was not feeling so ill.

I got out and dried on a stiff, rough towel, hurrying to get as soon as possible into my warm, woollen pyjamas.

"You'll wear a hospital night-shirt while you're here," laid the nurse, snatching my pyjamas from me and handing me a cold, hard, much-mended calico thing shaped like a pillow-case with one linen button at the neck. I put it on and found it only reached my knees.

"Now get into bed or you'll catch cold," she said.

"Say that again," I said through chattering teeth.

I asked where my hot-water-bottle, sponge, and writing-case had been put.

"No personal belongings in this ward," I was told.

"May I have a hospital hot-water-bottle?" I asked.

"We don't have them."

"How do I write letters without my case?" I was now repentantly thinking of writing to Donald to modify some of the adjectives I had thrown at him during our quarrel.

"You don't. This is a fever hospital. No letters are allowed."

I lay down between the icy sheets, hoping my fever would warm me. Suddenly I became too hot, but more with anger than with fever. How dare this chit of a nurse treat me like this? Then I saw that she had not even left me any water to drink, and I began to cry.

I was left alone for some hours until another nurse brought in a large plateful of congealed stew and a bowl of suet pudding.

"Can I have a glass of water?" I asked.

"Hoity toity, where d'you think you've come from? If you want to drink out of a glass you'd better go to the doctor's dining-room. You won't get one anywhere else." She looked at me more closely. "You've got quite a rash," she said. "I'll get you a mug."

"When do I see the doctor?"

"The doctor sees you when he feels like it."

I planned, when he came, to arrange my instant removal to my billet. Surely a doctor would understand that this was not a healthy place for anyone with German measles.

Hours later he came. He was a short, thick-set man. His greying, stubbly hair had a macabre white patch in it. He cast his eye over my extensive rash and swollen neck-glands with approval, but went out without bothering to answer any of my questions.

I was trapped, more surely than when I was confined in the cell guarded by two F.A.N.Y.s with, so the story went, fixed pen-knives. There had been something so funny about that episode that I was amused almost all through it. But there was nothing funny about this. I wondered what my legal position was. I had never been in any hospital before. Can a patient get up and walk out? Even if legally I could not, there was nothing to stop me. The white night-shirt would make excellent camouflage in the snow. But where could I go to?

A nurse brought my tea, a mug of thick, dark-brown fluid and four slices of bread with a dab of margarine on the plate and no knife to spread it.

"What? You haven't touched your dinner?" she exclaimed in surprise.

"All I want is cold water," I said.

"I'll see about it," she said, and did not.

I crawled out of bed with the mug of tea and took it out onto the veranda. I poured it over the balcony and then scooped up some snow in the empty mug and took it back to bed. But it would not melt. I crammed it into my mouth as it was. It helped.

Two nurses came in after dark to make my bed.

"You can get up and go along to the bathroom to wash," said one.

The nurses' feet had trodden the snow on the veranda into hard little balls of ice. My slippers had been taken away. But I went. Near the bathroom was the Sister's room. In it was a telephone. The room was empty. I went in and picked up the receiver.

"Telegrams, please," I said sharply, in the kind of voice I imagined a Sister would use.

To my relief I was switched straight through to Post Office Telegrams. But I could not be sure the hospital operator might not be hearing. I felt too cold and tired to try and think out anything cryptic, so, in school French, I spelled out, *"Je suis froid j'ai faim me cherchez vite Verily"*, trying to make it sound as much as possible like a list of rare drugs being ordered by somebody important In the hospital. I addressed it to Elizabeth, who was stationed ten miles away, and added the name of the hospital. I clumped the receiver down, suddenly feeling warm again, too warm. In fact I felt really hot.

I went triumphantly back to my cubicle, where the two nurses ignored me. They were discussing the colour of the hair of the soldier in the next cubicle. He had blackwater fever, from which he soon died.

* * * * *

In the middle of the night the Matron came in. She carried a huge basket of fruit and flowers, and put them down by my bed as though they were a present from herself. Elizabeth had wasted no time.

Next morning I was brought my dressing-gown and slippers, my pyjamas, my hot-water-bottle (filled), my writing-case (with my diary well thumbed), and my sponge.

"What's it for?" the nurse asked curiously, holding up the sponge.

"Washing with."

"We always use soap here."

Telegrams of condolence and bright encouragement came in, so I knew Elizabeth had been busy informing my family and friends. Her own telegram repeated, *"Keep a stiff upper lip for the honour of the Third."*

An alderman friend from a neighbouring city drove over in his sparkling Rolls Royce, with sweets for the nurses and a huge parcel of delicacies for me. The Matron lent me her own radio set. All this was very nice for me; but I could not help thinking of the other soldiers who would still die there of blackwater and other fevers, alone.

In a few days the German measles had subsided; but I had a really bad cold with uncomfortable earache. The doctor ignored these, and sent me the two hundred and seventy miles home on sick-leave. Meanwhile German measles swept through the forces, and soon cases were no more admitted to hospital than were cases of flea-bite.

The journey south produced most of the conditions necessary for a game of "reactions". Reactions was a game I often used to play on a long journey. From the look of the other passengers, you guess how they would react in a railway accident or other crisis that might fling them all together and pierce their normal reticence. We had no railway accident; but the journey, scheduled for five hours, because of the snow took fourteen. There was no heating in the carriage, and the cold was almost as biting as in my fever ward. This time, however, there was no need to guess reactions.

The ten, or so, occupants of the carriage drew together and sought comfort in conversation. Encouraged by a lively young Marine major, we shared sandwiches and played rummy with a pack of cards produced by an elderly naval rating. The major spread newspapers over our knees and, when that failed to warm us, passed round his flask of brandy. Only a sedate girl in civilian clothes refused to join in; but soon the cold and the long waits drove her to accept a warming sip. When at last we reached London, we felt we had been through so much together that it was almost painful to part. The Marine major and I were the last out onto the platform.

"Come on, Fanny," he said, "let's go into the hotel and have a civilised sandwich." He picked up my bag and carried it with his into the station hotel.

"First I must telephone some friends to see if I can spend the night with them," I said. "It's too late to get a train down to Sussex."

I telephoned Elizabeth's parents, who told me they could give me a bed for the night.

When I joined the major in the cocktail bar he seemed quite different from the life-and-soul of the railway carriage.

He looked younger and quieter. We sat down with sandwiches and drinks and exchanged life stories. He was twenty-five and the youngest of four brothers. He, too, was the child of a parson.

"I say, Fanny," he said suddenly, "I like you awfully. Will you marry me?"

I laughed.

"Honestly, I want to marry a nice girl like you that I can let my hair down with, and yet who looks all right in public. I expect I can get some sort of a job after the war—trying shoes on people or something."

"How nice of you," I said, "but—"

"Then will you come and dance with me at the Four Hundred tonight?"

"I'd love to, but I've already made a plan to go straight to some friends where I'm staying the night."

"Pity," said the major. He got me a taxi. "I'll be at my club. The Junior Carlton. Ring me in the morning. I'll want to know how you are. You seem to have forgotten you only came out of hospital today."

I had. The taxi crawled along the icy streets in the black-out, and I realised that neither of us knew what the other's real name was.

Next day I went on down to Sussex and arrived home with excruciating earache. I spent the next month in bed with severe ear trouble, while angry letters of complaint flew almost daily from Sussex to the fever hospital from my parents, doctors, and other well-wishers.

I struggled back to the F.A.N.Y.s in the north, still only half-recovered, and found I had been posted to London—at any rate temporarily.

Lucy's F.A.N.Y. unit was in London too. One afternoon I was having tea with her when a friend of hers came in. They began to talk about various men they knew who were crazy enough to set off with no proper equipment as international volunteers to join in the war in Finland.

"—and then another one is that tall, thin man with auburn hair who writes—Donald Anderson," the friend said.

Lucy looked up.

"You didn't tell me, V.," she said.

"Oh, didn't I?" I said, trying to sound vague. I felt myself going red; and a dreadful numbness seized me. I ceased to hear what they were saying. I turned the news over and over in my mind, hoping to find some aspect of it that I liked. Of course it was very brave of him to go, and I was proud of him for volunteering. But who was I to be proud of him? We had not met or exchanged letters since Boxing Day. Suddenly I panicked. It was bad enough that Donald, with his delicate chest and no woollen underwear, was going off into the Finnish snows; but that he could do so without telling me, and remain in the right, was a major catastrophe.

I left Lucy and her friend and went straight to Montagu's office.

Montagu, only ten minutes before, had become engaged to a very pretty girl. He was not in a receptive mood. As soon as his fiancée had left to tell her mother the news, I said urgently:

"Is it true Donald's going to Finland?"

"Yes, but what's the worry? It's all washed up, isn't it? You and him?"

"Who said so?"

"He did."

"When?"

"He got the idea you had other plans. A Marine major or somebody."

"A what?"

"A Marine major. Someone was saying in the club—"

"Oh, how silly!" I said, beginning to cry, to Montagu's acute embarrassment.

"Why cry?" he said gently.

"Because—because you're going to marry that awful girl," I said irrelevantly.

"Mm," agreed Montagu thoughtfully.

"I must go now," I said, mopping my eyes.

I hurried out into the black-out towards Donald's rooms in Half Moon Street. On a traffic island at Hyde Park Corner I began to cry again. What if it really was all washed up? But it was impossible. Donald would never allow it. I let my tears fall into a fire-bucket as the buses rolled by, thundering a kind of *Finlandia* in my ears.

Donald's rooms showed all too plainly that the Finnish rumour must be true. Trunks and suitcases full of clothes I had never seen before were open; and garments were strewn about the floor—riding breeches, a cummerbund, white duck suits, a cricket blazer, a polo helmet—but no woollen underwear. I sat down with it all and waited for him to come in.

I waited a long time. Gradually, sitting among his things, a calm came over me. Donald professed a contempt for personal belongings: yet all these things were well-loved, I could feel that. I touched his dressing-gown.

Then I took some blank pages out of the waste-paper basket and wrote him a long and rambling letter. A clock outside struck ten. I crumpled up all the pages and stuffed them into my respirator-case and went away.

The next day the Finnish war was over.

6

FRANCE HAS FALLEN, I read from a bus on a news-bill. It was a shock. Only a few weeks before, I had heard a radio talk by Somerset Maugham on the French war effort. In their factories and on their farms, it seemed, the French were setting us an example in drive and determination.

Then came the evacuation from Dunkirk. Ambulance drivers and hospital-train personnel, who had been waiting for nearly a year with nothing to do, were suddenly called on to work without a break until the several thousand wounded had been carried to appropriate hospitals throughout Britain. This was the time when at last there seemed some point in being a F.A.N.Y.

Ironically enough, I could do nothing. The ear infection which followed German measles had returned, and I spent most of the loveliest May I can remember in a military hospital in the Midlands. Aunt Evie and Beryl came to visit me in a ward of fifty A.T.S., where the treatment was considerably more humane than at the fever hospital. My mother came up from Sussex and took me to stay at Clifton with Aunt Evie until I was fit for the journey south.

Now, on sick leave at the rectory, I watched a solid slow-moving line of army trucks and ambulances on the Hastings road, as more and more men were landed on the Coast only a few miles away. Some of the famous "few" flew over on their way to and from giving their decisive air cover to the evacuation.

Angrily I listened to the distant rumbles of gunfire as I wandered uselessly about the rectory garden. My mother was out all day with the W.V.S., and my father was comforting the sick and dying at a military camp and did not even come back at night.

My mother came in to supper as chirpily as though she had been to a garden fête, and entertained me with stories of how the soldiers had received the W.V.S. tea and attention after their ordeal. Three of our village boys, she said, had rowed across the Channel in a small fishing-boat and had landed not far from home. She had seen them and conveyed the news to their families that they were alive. A fourth had been shot through the finger by machine-gun fire from the air as they pushed out the boat, and they had got him on board the hospital-ship I had known earlier in the war. Later we heard that the hospital-ship had been bombed by the Germans and the boy had lost a leg.

After two days of this I could bear my inactivity no longer.

"I'm going back," I told my mother.

"But you can't. You're on sick leave."

"I'm not sick now."

"They won't want you. You'll only be ill again and just be a nuisance. Besides, you'll take up a valuable seat in the train."

"I can sit on the floor," I said and changed into my uniform.

Reluctantly my mother drove me to the station.

I travelled north in a train full of evacuated soldiers, exhausted yet still garrulous. There was a competition in our carriage as to who had lost the most equipment. They had all left Dunkirk or the neighbouring sands with a relief that still showed in their faces.

"Ever slept all night on the *plage*, Fanny?" I was asked.

"Yes" I said.

"Ooo, and don't the sand itch you?" the soldier said delightedly.

I hoped my answer would be taken as a straight lie; for I wanted to hear what it was really like to sit on the edge of a continent for a day or two with the enemy behind you, not sure whether you would be killed or taken prisoner, fairly sure that you would not be got away. But, when they accepted me as one of themselves, they pushed those days and nights of terror into the backs of their minds as something to reserve for impressing their families with later, and got on with matters in hand.

"Come on, Fanny, what about joining us in a nice friendly game of solo?"

"No, pontoon," said another.

"Make it nap," said a third.

It served me right. I should now know less about it than their families.

I reported for duty to my last unit in the Midlands. There was such a flap on that nobody noticed I had come back at least a fortnight too soon. One rumour had it that the F.A.N.Y.s were to be armed against the expected Invasion. Meanwhile all road-worthy ambulances and cars were out driving the wounded.

I was told to change into overalls and, five minutes later, was in the garage binding an ignition cable with insulating tape. It was not driving, but I was content: soon one more ambulance could go out on the road.

A fortnight later, when the evacuation was complete and all the wounded were settled in hospital to recover or not, my mother telephoned me to say that orders had arrived at the rectory for me to attend a medical board at the nearby military hospital. I took the matter to my C.O., expecting her to have the orders cancelled, now that I was fit and back on duty. She was not friendly.

"You can't just walk in and out as you please," she said. "Of course you must go and attend the medical board."

"I'm fit for duty," I pointed out. In fact outstanding physical strength had been required of all of us during the last two weeks.

"That's not the point."

She made out a railway warrant.

At the medical board in Sussex, my ears were examined, poked into, and pressed from behind.

"Does that hurt?"

"No."

"This?"

"No."

"This?"

"No—yes," I edged away.

"Do you want to go back?"

"Of course."

"Then it does hurt. You'd better not go back yet."

"Oh, please—" I said.

"Oh, all right. You're fit enough otherwise. But there's still a bit of inflammation there."

Walking home to the rectory, I tried to analyse my reasons for wanting to go back. My heart had never been in the F.A.N.Y.s until Dunkirk. The community life did not suit me. Discipline did not appeal. I was not a good F.A.N.Y., either technically or socially. Could it be patriotism? Knowing myself, I felt there must be some more selfish motive behind it. Then I remembered telling Lucy I should feel safer right in the war.

That was it. Anything might happen now, not only to my brothers and friends in the navy, the army, the air force, but to my parents, to Rhalou with her little family, and to Lorema still at school. In the F.A.N.Y.s I should be safe from the impact. Somebody else does your thinking for you in the army, and even your feeling. And if I were killed, well, in the F.A.N.Y.s life was that much less interesting to want to cling on to.

I went into the kitchen where my mother was packing tins of sardines into a box, for burying in the garden to consume after the invaders, if any, had passed. But I knew at once that something had happened which was more personal to us than possibly enemy invasion. Erroll? No, he was in a shore job at Chatham recovering from a depth-charge. Merlin? My mother had already begun to tell me. It was Dear Steaming Kettle, missing believed killed. We had known him since he went to Dartmouth with Erroll, often in scrapes, often helping other people out of theirs, falling in and out of love as frequently as the submarines, which he loved best of all, dived and surfaced. Dear Steaming Kettle was part of life itself, and the least expected to be the first of the gang to go.

Yes, I must get back to the F.A.N.Y.s where thinking and feeling were done for you.

I telephoned my C.O. to say I had been passed fit: should I return by the next train? The answer was, "No, not here. You're not on our strength. You were struck off when you went into hospital two months ago. I don't know where you'll go. You must wait for orders."

Wait for orders! That meant I must stay at the rectory where every branch and bud in the garden reminded me of the days that could never again be the same, whatever happened now. No, it was impossible. I asked my mother to telephone me when my orders came, then I packed some clothes and went to London to stay with a cousin in Chelsea.

I arrived in the middle of a party. There were some old friends on leave and a few I had never met before. They were going on to dance at the Hungaria. I went too.

Next day there were no orders but more parties. An extraordinary mood of exultation sweetened the air of London at that time. Everything seemed against us. Scandinavia, Holland, Belgium, and France had fallen to the enemy. Italy had just declared war on us, and we had sustained enormous losses in material and fairly big losses in men at Dunkirk. And yet there was this strange soaring of spirits. Even the very colours of the summer seemed heightened, the sky bluer, the clouds whiter, and the darkness darker. The combined sense of danger and of unity was exhilarating.

It was inevitable that Donald and I should meet during those queer, dreamlike days, when everybody who lived or worked or went on leave in London was out and about. It was inevitable that all barriers would be swept aside in that atmosphere. We had seen each other at the Hungaria and exchanged a few cordial words. We met once again by chance and after that daily by design.

Donald was doing well at the Ministry of Information. He had an interesting and quite difficult job. He had also formed a Home Guard company to defend the Senate House, the strongest building in Bloomsbury. But that was not enough. Having been foiled in his efforts to fight for the Finns, he was now trying to become a rear-gunner in the R.A.F.

"They don't mind my age," he said. "It's not a skilled job. You just have to be able to shoot."

The death-rate of rear-gunners was high. But now I ceased to feel selfishly about Donald's desire to be right in the war. Even I knew this passion, without having been a professional soldier for years as he had been.

No orders came for me and I felt more and more non-existent. There was a song being played by dance bands at that time, "I'm nothing but a nothing. I'm not a thing at all". I believe it was about a bat; but it was just how I felt when everybody else was so busy or else on such very short leave.

One evening I drifted down to Chatham to visit Erroll and his wife and their baby of three weeks old. I travelled by motor-coach to save a few pence on the fare. The sun shone on the green fields, and it was pleasing to see how well defended they were against enemy airborne landings, reminding me of the pages of my first French reading-book. A car, a hayrake, an old kitchen range, a bedstead, a harrow were dotted about one field. Posts and wires had been erected to wreck aircraft trying to land on the roads. A steam-engine and a hay-wagon were piled up with old chairs to form a road barrier, which could quickly be closed by a nearby tractor.

I found Erroll and Daphne in a little house on a ridge. Lorema was staying with them. The secure sight of the new baby in his cradle made everything I had seen and heard in London, and on the way here, seem like some fantasy in a film. Only the baby with his young mother and father was real and lasting.

After supper Lorema and I went out to telephone home. We stood in the narrow passage of a neighbouring house, waiting for the call to come through. From the front room we could hear Churchill's voice broadcasting, "We are fighting by ourselves alone. Here in this strong City of Refuge we await the impending assault. Perhaps it will come tonight. Perhaps it will come next week. We must show ourselves capable of meeting a sudden violent shock." His likening of the British Isles to a "strong City of Refuge" struck me with a strange kind of pleasure.

I talked to my father. Still there were no orders for me.

I quoted Donald on the ways of War Office clerks.

"You're not seeing *him* again?" my father said in a tone of rebuke.

"Why not?" And we launched into one of those family arguments which go on and on and effect nothing, except to leave both sides angry. Lorema was drawn into it at my end, and my mother at the other.

After Churchill's broadcast I wanted my orders desperately, so I suppose I would have been angry anyway.

Lorema and I went to bed early. We talked for a while.

"I can't think what they've got against Donald," I said bitterly.

"Nor can I," Lorema said sleepily. "He's sweet."

"I shan't tell them when I see him again," I said and went to sleep.

A tremendous bang woke us, followed by the swooping sound of a diving aeroplane. There were two more even louder thumps, and Lorema and I sat up in bed, surprised not to feel frightened. Erroll came in, moving more quickly than I had ever seen him move before, and yet giving the impression of moving and talking without haste.

"We'll go to the public air-raid shelter. Bring your respirators." He went down to turn off gas and water.

A siren soared up to its full howl, and others took up the tune. "Perhaps it will come tonight," Lorema repeated.

We both shuffled into shoes and threw on a few clothes and went in to Daphne. She smiled and picked up her baby. She wrapped him in a blanket and went downstairs where Erroll was holding the family's respirators, which included the huge iron-lung apparatus provided for babies.

I took a childish pleasure in being the last downstairs: somehow it helped my hurt feelings over my lack of recall.

In bright moonlight we ran down the side of the ridge. It was a run I shall never forget, with the drama of the yawling brawling sirens sounding in our ears, and the dark shapes chasing across the face of the moon, and the much nearer danger of the pot-holes beneath our feet. But I was grateful to Erroll for letting us run; he might have insisted on our walking sedately while the occupants of the other houses tore past us. With his uniform jacket over his pyjamas, he carried the baby and its respirator. His unbrushed curls pushed out from under his uniform cap and gave him a happy look.

We reached the ramp down to the shelter.

"One minute, twenty-five seconds," Erroll informed us, looking at his watch. And yet, as in a motor accident or other occurrence when the nerves are tensed up, so much seemed to have happened, with details standing out so clearly, since the first bomb fell.

The shelter was long and dark and damp. It had not been used before. We shelterers had yet to learn the value of warm clothes, bedding, hot drinks, and snacks for a long night of waiting. There were no seats; and at first we stood up and listened to the various ways in which our fellows had been affected by the first explosion.

"I went all of a shake."

"It fair turned me up."

"I said to my hubby. 'It makes you think you can do with a cup of tea after that lot.'"

"Our houses aren't no good. They wasn't built for it."

But there was no doubt about it, they were enjoying themselves. The spirit of the strong City of Refuge had touched us all.

Daphne sat down against the wall with her baby, and Erroll stood beside them. Soon Lorema and I sat down close together, for it was cold now. We took it in turns to hold the well-wrapped baby to warm our hands. The grumble of guns faded and there was a long silence.

The alert lasted four hours. Then we knew the glorious relief of the all-clear, a relief that, we were to find in days to come, was more often from cold dragging boredom than from the crash and excitement of falling bombs.

"We'll dig our own shelter for next time," said Erroll; and later I heard that they spent the following five nights with the baby in a slit trench in the garden.

Back in London next morning I found frantic messages left by my mother with friends, telling me that my orders had come. I was posted back to the depot near Clifton.

I lunched with Donald. The R.A.F. had found his breathing to be faulty for high altitudes. We both felt I had been lucky to be in the first raid on England, about which of course there was already much talk, although the public was not told till much later that Chatham had been the objective. I described it in detail to Donald, and added part of my telephone conversation with my father.

"So I'm still spoiling your chances," he said.

"No, no, no," I said, "you're not."

"Would you—with your extravagant tastes—like being married to a poor man?"

"That," I said, getting up and slinging on my respirator case, for I should have to hurry if I was going to catch my train, "only depends on who he is."

He kissed me out on the pavement in Soho, and I was quite sure I should like being married to a poor man.

"Write at once and let me know your address," he said with a pleasurable urgency.

7

Now, LESS THAN a fortnight later, I had walked out of the F.A.N.Y.s to marry Donald. With Montagu and Lorema as witnesses, we entered into the ceremony with a seriousness of which I had not known I was capable.

"Remember God. Remember each other," said the doctor of divinity who married us. "You have lived for yourselves. Now you must sink yourselves and live for each other."

That was when I looked back. Selfish, frivolous, and unreliable, I vowed to do better now that I had some real aim in life.

The four of us came out of church smiling and happy, and turned into Green Park to walk under the trees and sort out our new relationships. Three Australian soldiers recognised our happiness and wished us luck.

For our honeymoon, Donald and I caught a slow meandering train to a village in Sussex that I had admired as a child. In the sixteenth-century inn where we had booked a room, we drank each other's health in the public bar. Labourers were beginning to collect round the darts board with mugs of beer.

"Darling, you look almost perfectly happy," I heard.

"I am. I am."

"Telephone for Mrs. Anderson," said the proprietress.

"That's you, darling."

"So it is."

I went to the telephone on the wall of the kitchen stairs.

"Just rang up to send you all our love and congratulations!" It was my mother, gay and enthusiastic, the quickest forgiver in the world. "I've just been arranging to plant out your spring vegetables. You'll need them in London. And now you're out of uniform, don't you think you ought to have a proper warm winter coat? I'll come up to London to see about it. Everybody sends their love. Lorema's just come down from London to tell us all about the wedding. She said you looked so pretty."

I went back to Donald.

"I dunno," I said with a sigh. "I don't deserve *any* of it, let alone the lot."

* * * * *

The F.A.N.Y.s were less forgiving. A telegram was forwarded from a London address, "RETURN TO DUTY IMMEDIATELY OR YOUR DISCHARGE NOT CONSIDERED."

"Decent of them to consider considering it," said Donald, who had hitherto not quite approved of the barefacedness of my desertion. The F.A.N.Y.s were not subject to military law, we had discovered.

"They didn't want me when I went back," I reminded him. "The first thing they did was to send me on forty-eight hours' leave."

"Which you enjoyed."

"I loved being at Clifton and thinking about you from the rose garden. But it wasn't war work."

"And this is?" We were lounging on deck-chairs in the garden of the inn.

"Of course it is, darling," I said emphatically. "If I can make you happy, you'll do your job at the Ministry better. Then we'll win the war."

Donald's family showed some signs of healthy curiosity in me. His elder sister and her husband asked us to lunch at the Cavalry Club. I went dressed to kill, which was just as well, for the exceptionally good-looking feminine counterpart of Donald, who greeted me in the club's drawing-room, was clothed with faultless taste and correctness.

My mind was prepared for an ordeal by inquisition, such as, in my own family, was inflicted on any girls that my brothers showed enough interest in to bring home. "Are you one of a large family?" my mother would begin. She would go on with, "Have you done things?" That meant, have you had a job and if so describe it?

So I first faced Blanche and Tom with an assortment of answers ready in my mind.

They threw me completely off my balance by not asking one single question from the beginning of lunch to the end. Yet it was a friendly meal, with bright general talk from Blanche and brotherly badinage from Tom.

"I thought you had more self-control, old boy," was his frivolous comment to Donald on our marriage.

Neither he nor Blanche seemed to appreciate the privilege they were permitted to enjoy in being connected with Donald.

And I, in my ignorance of other families' codes of behaviour, was upset that my new relations should find me so undeserving of interest. The only fact I learned from them about themselves—and this was in answer to a direct question from me—was where their children, a son and a daughter, were at school.

A few weeks after this meeting I went to Winchester on an errand for my mother. Her own ageing governess was ill and had to be moved into a nursing home. My mother could not go herself, but wanted the old lady to feel she was still revered by the family.

With that job behind me, I thought I might as well take my new nephew out to tea. I had helped to take little boys—or men, as they call themselves—out from the College before, and I knew that the great thing was food, never mind the conversation. I called on Geoffrey's housemaster, and somewhat reluctantly he sent for the boy.

As soon as Geoffrey came into the room I realised that my eyes had been directed at too low a level. Instead of the roly-poly little schoolboy I was expecting, a tall, rather sophisticated young man-about-town strolled in.

"This young lady says she's your aunt," his housemaster accused him, rather suspiciously, "and she would like to take you out to tea."

Of course Geoffrey had no idea who I was, but thought he would like to go out; so he claimed me without further investigation.

He took me to a comfortable hotel where I found that, with him, the great thing was conversation, though we did have a drink together. We talked hunting and dances and people we both knew, and before we parted he asked me who I really was.

*   *   *   *   *

Next time Donald had leave we went up north to combine his shooting partridges on a friend's estate with my being hauled over the coals by the F.A.N.Y.s. This turned out to be a very ladylike affair. Nobody really wanted me back, but the honour of the corps needed to look unblemished. I was told in the orderly room to produce a medical certificate stating that I was unfit for service.

Next day I went out with the guns and followed Donald, dog-like, over fields and fences.

"Who's that healthy young woman who's been striding out with us all morning?" I heard an elderly gun ask at lunch.

"Donald's new wife, Doctor," our host replied.

The word "doctor" made me prick up my ears. I boldly asked him for a medical certificate.

Without hesitating he pushed his wine-glass to one side and took from his pocket a pen and a writing-pad. "You must tell me some disease or disability," he said with a smile.

I recollected some of the jargon from the medical board. He handed me a scribbled note, which did the trick with the F.A.N.Y.s.

* * * * *

We arrived back in London on a Saturday afternoon and parted at the station to meet again at tea-time. Donald might have been setting out to cross the Sahara instead of St. James's Park, so strong was the pang in my heart as I watched him disappear out of sight. I went by Underground to Sloane Square. As I emerged I found myself being hurried into a doorway by an excited air-raid warden.

"Didn't you hear the siren?" he said.

"No. I was in the tube."

"Then look up there," he said.

A swarm of shining gnat-like planes moved slowly in the sky, with little puffs of what looked like cotton wool below them.

"That's the Luftwaffe," he said, pulling me out of the doorway and into the next in an effort to get me to his shelter. "And that's our gunfire falling short. Listen to it."

Oh my goodness, I thought. They're heading straight towards Half Moon Street. I could not bring myself to go down into the shelter until I saw them turn.

"Now they'll be going for the docks," the air-raid warden said.

It was September 9th, and this, with five hundred planes, was the biggest daylight raid the German air force ever attempted.

* * * * *

After that it was easy in central London to find a flat within our means. The rents of all top-floor flats dropped with an almost audible thud. For two pounds a week, a luxurious little unfurnished flat, closely carpeted and just off Berkeley Square, was ours. It backed on to a monastery.

Between us, Donald and I had just enough furniture to make it attractive and comfortable. The only thing we bought was an enormous six-foot-by-six-foot double divan, which we had made for us at great expense. It was probably the most impossible piece of furniture either of us had ever slept on, but we were too polite to say so. It rose up in a rounded ridge in the middle; and, because it had no headboard, the pillows as well as the inhabitants had a continual struggle against the laws of gravity.

Far more comfortable was a single mattress that I laid in one corner of the cellar, seven stories down. As the blitz grew heavier, more and more of our nights were spent in that cellar, which we shared with several other people, including some bombed-out families whose only home it was. Our landlady hung curtains up to try and create an impression of privacy. But when a bomb dropped particularly near and the old walls rocked and you could hear them crumbling inside, like sooty chimneys on a windy night, we all drew in breath as one man.

Thick wedges of glass let into the pavement allowed the flickering light of incendiary bombs to filter in when they fell. Donald could never resist these, and would dash out in his dressing-gown to help the firemen throw sand on them. When the church attached to the monastery was fired, he and the priest in charge, unable to do anything, stood in the porch merely to admire the beauty of the pillars against the flames.

After a long and stimulating day in the Ministry, Donald worked with zeal at training and commanding his Home Guard company, often staying on duty with them all night. Yet he still came home in bubbling spirits and agreed to go down to the cellar only to oblige me. One noisy night he said, "Stick by me, darling, and we'll both be all right. I'm immortal."

By day, for no reason at all, I felt quite safe in the flat during raids. A miniature staircase led from our glass-roofed hall up to the roof that we shared with the monastery. During the raid I would rush up there to make sure that the tall white blocks of the Ministry of Information—with Donald inside—were still standing. But I had to take care to respect the monastic vows and not step on their part of the roof, where women had been repudiated.

During an early daylight raid I became one of the first casualties to be treated by the first-aid post set up in the garage under Berkeley Square. I was making shepherd's pie in our small kitchen, carefully following the recipe book because I had never learnt to cook before I was married. A bomb dropped some way off. The vibration caused a heavy saucepan to bounce off a high shelf; it hit and broke a beer bottle on a lower shelf, which then fell on my head. It was the silliest accident, because anyone in their senses would have looked down and not up while that sort of thing was going on. I went on with my shepherd's pie till I realised that the excess of uncooked gravy was dropping from my head.

When I asked the local chemist for lint and disinfectant, he felt it was only fair to allow the first-aid post to claim me. He personally led me down their ramp; and immediately a label with my name and address and religion on it was tied round my arm in case I died during treatment. The V.A.D.s were as pleased to see the blood running down my face as we, in the F.A.N.Y.s, were when a new old crock fell into our hands. Half a dozen V.A.D.s made a rush at me and treated my small abrasion as though my whole head had been blown off. They treated me for shock with sugared tea, specially brewed, and they would have gladly carried me away on a stretcher had I allowed it.

Shelter life in Mayfair was curiously mixed up with the usual expensive night life, for restaurants and dancing had all gone underground. One Saturday night we went to bed early with colds. A raid had begun, so we were down in the cellar. But Donald became restless, and so at about nine, when the all-clear sounded, we got up and went out on to the pavement for air. There we met two friends on leave from the navy. As soon as the sirens sounded again, they assured us that London was much more terrifying than bombing at sea, and insisted on dragging us down the nearest steps, which led to a restaurant where a dance orchestra gently drowned the sounds of war above. Women in long evening dresses were dancing with men in uniform; waiters were serving roast chicken and French wines. Except that the room was hot and we could not take off our coats because we wore only pyjamas under them, it was a very good evening and our hosts returned with us afterwards to our cellar for the rest of the night.

Soon we had so many regular passing guests on leave that we brought down another mattress for our "spare shelter".

When we were alone during an alert, we played word-games or read aloud to each other by the light of a candle stuck in a bottle. Donald read me the whole of the Song of Solomon during a silence between a period of droning and diving planes (which other shelterers were claiming as "ours" or "theirs") and a more violent one of bursts of gunfire and the whistling and crash of falling bombs.

For weeks the alerts lasted all night, the all-clear sounding regularly soon after dawn. Then Donald and I would climb up the seven flights of stairs to our flat, sweep up any glass or china that might have been broken, and have breakfast by the gas-fire—provided the gas was still coming through. If it were not, I boiled the kettle over little sticks of solid methylated on a trivet arranged in the sink from forks and spoons.

At that time of day I was at my lowest. Air-raids, like bad nights with a teething child, pile up against you. Lack of sleep increases one's impatience with further lack of sleep, and creates worry and fear.

Sometimes I was so frightened during night raids that I left the cellar and climbed upstairs to be sick.

"I don't think it's fear," said Donald one morning, when I confessed my weakness.

"Of course it is, darling," I said lightly. "Do you like salmon?" I changed the subject.

"I adore it."

I went out and bought a beautiful cut and some salad. I had dealt with tinned salmon and smoked salmon before, but this was going to be much better. It was fresh Scotch. I arranged it all charmingly on a tray and carried it down to the cellar all ready for Donald when he came in to supper.

"D'you think you've cooked it quite long enough?" he asked when he saw it.

"Cooked it? You don't cook salmon," I said; and I hadn't. I toiled up to the flat again and found that Mrs. Beeton recommended a fish-kettle. We had no fish-kettle, so I threw it into a saucepan and boiled it hard and fast. A bomb whistled down and I turned the gas up even higher. Another came down, and I turned the gas off, snatched the saucepan from the stove, and ran down the stairs, colliding with Donald who had come up to see if I was happy.

We ate the salmon in the cellar. It was rather soggy and pale, but tasted all right.

We spent the week-ends making the flat homey, which often entailed doing the same task more than once. Donald would spend one Sunday afternoon fitting reinforced talc into windows which had had their glass blown in; then a week later he would do the same job again after the talc had been blown out.

One day I was having a bath with the gas-geyser roaring away, drowning all other sounds, when I was amazed to see it slide down the wall into the bath with me. Somehow it seemed indecent, and I got out embarrassed. It had been shaken from the wall by an explosion in Piccadilly.

The flat remained in workable repair for long enough for us to give a respectably-sized party. We were delighted by the number of guests who turned up. People were not keen on going visiting at that time, because of the difficulty of getting home afterwards. Some of the more luxurious hotels provided for this difficulty with comfortable beds in their cellars, silk eiderdowns and attendant valets.

When we dined in friends' houses we usually went equipped to stay the night. One friend we often dined—and breakfasted— with was the mother of our shooting host in the north, at whose table I got the medical certificate that released me from the F.A.N.Y.s. Molly, who had been used to a full and extremely comfortable social life, was now a whole-time air-raid warden. In addition, on her resting days she worked at a bench in an ordnance factory. The courage and stamina that she showed would have been highly creditable in a much younger woman. When the war was over, Donald said she deserved a special medal. Since the Government were slow about giving her one, Donald did. It was a handsome silver piece, with an impression of St. Paul's Cathedral in an air-raid. He got the jeweller to record round its rim that Molly "swerved not from her chosen duty, while peril was all around."

One afternoon I set out before dark to dine with her. I walked across the park with our night-things in a bag, skirting the wide areas where unexploded bombs had been roped off.

"Darling," Molly explained over a delicious dinner when we had exchanged our news, "I shall have to put you to sleep in another room tonight because there are two unexploded bombs in the garden, chained together in some mysterious manner."

She had been down the hole to look at them but could not recognise their type.

Bombs with delayed explosion were now a favourite trick of the Germans.

A few nights later we were woken soon after three in the morning on our cellar mattress. A policeman was flashing his torch over us.

"Orders to clear the houses in this street immediately," he said. "There's a time-bomb on the corner."

I thought of our dear little flat up above and felt how disloyal we should be if we left without having one last look at it. We went up and found it more charming than ever, now that it was possibly within minutes of total destruction.

We wondered which of our possessions we ought to save. Anything we took would have to be carried in our hands. A valuable water-colour from the wall? The manuscript of the latest play? Armfuls of clothes? The policeman fidgeted anxiously at our debate. But somehow all lasting material things seemed to have lost their importance. Donald took his last cigar. I took the bunch of grapes my mother had sent the day before from the rectory hot-house.

On the way down I ran a little.

Now that we were fully awake and out in the street, we felt disinclined to follow the policeman and his flock into the cellars of the American Embassy. On such occasions I am apt to think up all kinds of less simple alternatives.

"Just as you like, darling," said Donald affably, lighting his cigar. His eye-glass dangled on a silk cord from round his pyjama-collar. "It's a warm night."

We walked up Davies Street towards a friend's house on the other side of Oxford Street. There were huge fires everywhere, which partially accounted for the warmth.

We were not the only pedestrians abroad that night in bedroom clothes. A man passed us striding purposefully along in a turkish bath-robe. A girl in a flowery kimono attached herself to us for company. We reached Oxford Street. To our right John Lewis's store blazed with giant fingers of red and yellow reaching for the raiders in the sky. On our left the Westbourne River had been released from its tunnel and was pouring torrents into the basement of a newly bombarded shoe-shop. Falling splinters from our gunfire made us move quickly into the entrance of a shop.

"Have you ever noticed," said the girl, "what a lot of glass there is in Oxford Street? If it isn't windows it's mirrors."

All the side streets out of Oxford Street were impassable. The girl said good-night and went towards Marble Arch. We turned back, deciding to head for some other friends, much further away, near Belgrave Square.

Firelight and moonlight made the night as bright as day. In Down Street we saw a wave of aircraft cross the face of the moon. Then a bomb whistled down. I pulled Donald under a porch. He pointed out with mild amusement that not only its roof but its walls were of glass.

The church where we were married stood black and strong-looking across the street. Donald started to lead me towards it. A clatter of anti-aircraft fire made me try to drag him back to the porch.

"Come on," he said brightly, holding me more firmly. We hurried across the street and into the church. We reached it just as the second and third bombs of that stick dropped almost simultaneously very near, with a tumbling, almost stunning, crash.

The aircraft passed and we came out from our guardian church. The glass porch further up the street had disappeared. Where it had stood was a mound of rubble.

We reached Green Park before the next wave of planes came over, and went into a dug-out where some bus-drivers had been all night. But there was no comfort in the cold earthy walls, so we came out before all the planes had passed. If we move from tree to tree, I thought insanely, they won't see us. Crossing Hyde

Park Corner without trees or doorways, therefore, became a challenge.

We found that our friends were away; but the hall porter of their block of flats recognised us and let us in. He wanted us to go down to the shelter; but I was tired of war. I wanted a proper bed and sleep.

Next morning our host looked into his flat on his way from the country to his office.

"Good Lord!" he said, and quoted the tag, "Ain't you got no 'omes to go to?"

"Probably not," we said; and he set about providing us with clothes to go out in.

Donald went off to the Ministry and our host drove me to our street, part of which we could see from a long way off had been laid low. Near a police barrier, which closed the street, the postman had laid out the street's letters on the pavement. There was a censored letter from Merlin, which might have come from any part of the world. One big corner of Berkeley Square looked as though it had been bitten off like a piece of crumbly cake. Wallpaper and light-fittings were bared to the public above the tumble of broken masonry and tangled pipes. A child's red shoe lay in the road, exposed and painfully moving.

I showed my identity card to the policeman guarding the barrier and he let me pass. Our block was intact, except for chimneys and windows. It was almost more of a shock to find the flat virtually in as good condition as we had left it, than it would have been to find it demolished. I had got used to the idea of seeing it no more.

Again I took up my work on the flat. There were still some more curtains to be made. I bought the material in Oxford Street, which was barely recognizable. Walls and buildings never seen before by the passer-by were revealed. Rubble and broken glass covered the pavements and much of the road. Smoke was still rising from the charred skeleton of John Lewis's. On and on the damage reached, away into the distance. It was too much to take in, too much to bear.

Yet in a few days, I knew now from experience, the mess would be cleared tidily away. Hoardings would be erected across the bare spaces with their newly revealed secrets. Plate-glass windows would be replaced in the shops by boards with small peep-through windows in the middle. But how could the frames of burnt buildings be toned down from their bleak attitude of despair to fit into the new make-do-and-mend Oxford Street?

On the way home I stepped into a telephone-box to tell Donald about the flat. Our own telephone, as well as gas and water, was out of action. While I was dialling the number, the sirens began to wail and then I saw a curious sight. An errand boy in the street wobbled and fell off his bicycle for no apparent reason, then, one by one, the awnings outside the shops between him and my telephone-box rose and fell. Only after that did I hear the explosion of the bomb that caused it.

"What about your going to Lucy for a few days?" Donald said on the telephone. Lucy was recovering from an operation on her knee in a cottage on her family's estate in the Cotswolds.

"But why? The flat's all right after all."

"I know. But you're not. You look awful and you keep on being sick."

"It's only fright. Did you see in the papers about the girl who died of shock when the sirens went for the fifth time that day? It's quite natural, you see."

"All the more reason for going to Lucy."

"I can't leave you. I don't want to, either."

"I shall be on Home Guard duty all tonight and most of tomorrow night."

"All right. And you come to Lucy's for the week-end."

While I was at Paddington Station that afternoon, the sirens sounded for the fifth time. I did not die of shock but I was sick again.

I was relieved when the train moved out and away beyond the sordid sights of destruction. I relaxed and sat back. Just then an aeroplane swooped down, and I was amazed to hear the rattle of a machine-gun and the spatter of bullets on the roof of the train, above its own sound. My fellow-passengers and I all agreed that we were too surprised to think of diving under the seats, as we should have done. An eager friendliness broke out among us and we exchanged bomb stories of the night before. Nobody really wanted to hear the others' stories, but each wanted to tell his own. Looking back now on the other passengers' bombs, they all fell so much nearer than my own, that I wonder I dared to compete. Buried all night, auntie dug out from under the water-tank, walls collapsing in the kitchen, flames a hundred feet high from burst gas-mains! How commonplace our night seemed in comparison.

At Moreton-in-Marsh it seemed clear that Lucy had not got my telegram saying I was coming, or else she was away. Her cottage, twenty-four miles from the station, was not on the telephone.

All my feeling of sickness returned now. It was cold and dark. I went into the inn near the station, and sat there too tired even to order myself a drink or a sandwich.

An old man roused me by prodding my arm.

"There's a lady in the lobby. Maybe she's for you."

I jumped up and rushed out to find Lucy by the door, brown and grinning, her fair hair untidy and comfortingly un-F.A.N.Y.-like.

* * * * *

My telegram had been delivered a few minutes before my train was due, and she had driven as hard as she could through the black-out to meet me. Neither speed nor darkness had ever held any fears for Lucy, as well I learned on summer holidays when I had dithered on a cliff-edge while she jumped down into some black cave.

"Is Donald well?" Lucy asked. "Don't talk about London. The whole thing terrifies me."

How brave I felt, particularly now I was out of it.

"Stop! Quick!" I said, when we had gone a little way. "I'm going to be sick."

"V!" exclaimed Lucy, with evident delight. "Why didn't you tell me?"

"Tell you what?"

"About being sick. I hope it's a boy. It might have red hair like Donald's."

"It's not a baby," I said pompously. "It's just sheer fright." But Lucy had convinced me. Before, I just couldn't believe anything so wonderful could happen to us, but now that Lucy had said it, I knew that it could.

"A girl would be marvellous too," I said slowly.

8

DONALD CAME DOWN for the week-end. The prospect of fatherhood made him more excited than I had ever seen him. We walked and frolicked together in the sunlight of those few late September days; such warm autumn sunlight it was. Burnished gold splashes of colour and red gold foliage were about us. Mushrooms nestled in the grass, which was still vividly green. Beach leaves still shone greenly with a silvery sheen in shafts of sunlight.

Donald and Lucy persuaded me to stay on for a week after he had gone back to London.

I took the village bus into the town, fourteen miles away, to buy a handbook about babies. I sat in a café reading it and thinking about all the dresses and nightgowns and bonnets I would make for my baby, a pleasure that Donald referred to later with approval as "the young sow tearing up her bedding." I pored over the pages in the book on pregnancy, as the bus joggled home. It stopped frequently to allow the driver to deliver a parcel or a library book he had changed. I began to enjoy the frightful nausea which swept over me in waves. It was not fear.

When I left Lucy I was in an elated mood. With her magical talent for making a holiday out of anything, she had made me smile inwardly on my good fortune.

I sat by the open carriage window eating shrimps, an inspiration of Lucy's against travel—and other—sickness.

The country was too beautiful for me to read Socrates, with which Lucy had also furnished me in one of her efforts to improve my mind. There were rainbows and golden lights about the bronzed trees which still carried their summer shapes. A little girl ran among a herd of cattle, waving her arms and successfully causing a bullock to skip into a gateway.

But with the first signs of return to the bombardment areas, a cold draught seemed to pass through me. Where a row of houses had stood when I went down to the Cotswolds, a stretch of broken bricks now lay. Far more than in central London, the laying bare of the privacy of the little houses seemed so sordid and cruel. I felt ashamed and turned my eyes away.

In the short time I had been out of London, I made myself believe that I had exaggerated the damage in my mind. Now I saw that it was all too true. A sadness came over me, but still no fear.

The rain, at first a light spatter, now fell heavily. As we steamed through the suburbs of London I seemed to grow a harder shell, and gradually became indifferent to the changes I saw. I could now observe dispassionately that a lower storey might be demolished while part of the roof remained untouched.

At Paddington Station I began to panic because Donald was not there. The train was an hour late. Then, as the crowd thinned, I saw him and I ran, not noticing the weight of my suitcase.

We took a taxi. An air battle broke out overhead, but we took no notice. The driver pulled back the window.

"Want to go down a shelter?" he asked.

"No, thanks," said Donald, "unless you do."

"It'll be double fare if I don't," said the driver.

"And double fare if he does," I said. "Let's go on."

I asked Donald why he had come out without a coat.

"The club was bombed. It was in the cloakroom."

"Then those thank-you letters for wedding presents have gone too. Serves me right for not posting them ages ago. I'll have to write them again. Now I can tell people about the baby."

"In the same letter?"

"Why not?"

"Because they'll either think you're very late in thanking them for wedding presents, or else you're very early in having a baby. Some people might think both."

"Because of our funny wedding?"

"It was a wonderful wedding. You showed courage. I love your courage. Look at it now!"

"Yes, I'm glad it wasn't all fear. I felt such a mug thinking I was as frightened as all that."

* * * * *

The pregnancy was confirmed at the local ante-natal clinic; and I came home proud to have booked a bed for the beginning of May at the Westminster Hospital.

A month later the maternity block of the Westminster Hospital was demolished. Most of the mothers seized their babies and managed to escape unhurt. One, whom I met in another hospital years later, told me she was trapped under a girder a few hours before her baby was due to be born. She showed me scars on her back from broken glass.

The maternity unit was re-established in a beautiful old Georgian house in Surrey, with a delightful high-walled garden. But the place was really quite unsuitable for a hospital.

I got to work on tiny garments. The bombing, though as intense as ever, no longer worried me. When Donald had flu I gave up insisting on our going down to the cellar at night. I had discovered that he ignored it while I was away and always slept in the flat.

Sometimes during a raid, when we were in the flat, because sounds came so much more clearly than down in the cellar, I would stand still, unable to move or speak or even breathe until some whistling bomb had exploded. But I was not really frightened. Once, while I was carrying soup to Donald in bed, I was struck immobile by the sound of an aeroplane not very far away coming down out of control. As soon as it had crashed I could go on. Next day we learned from the little old daily help we had acquired, that it was an enemy plane which had crashed in flames with a load of explosives on the railway lines leading out of Victoria Station. She lost her home as a result.

Somehow the winter passed. I found it steadily harder and harder work to climb up the seven flights of stairs with a full shopping-basket. But I was proud of my swanky maternity clothes, which made me look more like a mountain than ever. Donald was proud of my burgeoning outline.

The authorities at the ante-natal clinic told me that they liked their expectant mothers to prepare themselves for their ordeal with a month away from air-raids. The Mothers were accommodated in a large house at Woking. This plan also cut down last-minute rushes to the evacuated hospital.

Montagu was now married and had taken a cottage in that part of Surrey. He offered to lend it to us for Easter. Our only responsibility was to feed hay to his wife's horse.

The horse was easily dealt with. Fat as I was, a pitchforkful of hay was not difficult for me to heave across a Cow-yard. The cottage was undoubtedly a dream one. Our room had a definite view. The birds in the trees woke us at dawn. ("Noisy brutes," said Donald sleepily.) In the evenings a log fire burned drowsily in the open grate. Fortunately there was a perfectly normal gas-cooker and water supply.

It was springtime, and the sheep were already well ahead of me with their lambs. For our daily exercise, Donald pushed me up a steep bank on to a splendid open heath.

The thought of joining those other expectant mothers for a month was worse than contemplating going back to school or back into the F.A.N.Y.s. A dreadful depression descended on me when I packed my suitcase, ticking off items on a printed list, just like school or the F.A.N.Y.s. I ran downstairs to Donald.

"I can't go. I can't go!" I said.

"I'll come with you," Donald soothed me. "Then, if we don't like the look of it, you can come back to London with me."

Together we went to Woking. It was easy to identity my destination. Women of all sizes and colours, but only one shape, were dragging themselves up a steep incline to a large modern mansion labelled, incongruously, *The Barrens*.

It was a fine house with flowering bulbs bordering the drive, which wound steeply up to its front door, leaving its inmates breathless and exhausted long before they reached it.

"What magnificent tulips," Donald pointed out brightly.

"It's a long way from the station," I puffed.

"I shall come and see you on Sunday," he said firmly, leaving me on the doorstep with no more talk about my going back to London. I felt like a child being dumped at its first kindergarten.

A coach stopped at the foot of the drive and disgorged that week's crop of London mothers. I waited for them to toil up the drive. Then we all went in together.

* * * * *

We *mothers*, as we were in many cases prematurely called, slept in large dormitories and ate our meals at long trestle tables exactly as we did in the more fashionable F.A.N.Y.s. We were presided over by an attractive and extremely efficient young warden. There was a pleasant feeling of freedom about the place: rules did not seem necessary, and we carried out the cooking and housework according to a rota without any daily orders. The warden soon discovered that my standard in all departments was lower than most, so I was put on permanently to dry up, at which she probably felt that I could do little damage except by dropping a few plates. I liked it in the scullery and made a lot of friends there. I found The Barrens, on the whole, more interesting than the F.A.N.Y.s. The complex mechanism of our well-filled bellies was less dull to discuss than the engines of F.A.N.Y. ambulances. My companions were certainly more interesting, perhaps because all had, or had had, husbands or lovers.

When our work was done we were free to wander into the town (where we met our husbands on Sundays) or to sit and knit in the common-rooms or dormitories, continuing our technical conversations from the previous meal.

"That cough you've got's due to baby. You'll see. Curls all over, 'e'll be. Bound to 'ave a lot of 'air with a cough like that."

"My auntie's friend, she came all out in a rash Wednesday. She's not been expecting long neither."

"You can tell. Mark my word. All out at the back like that's bound to be a boy."

We had only one subject, but we gave it infinite variety.

The last month of pregnancy is always a slow one. Life at The Barrens moved only slightly slower, but was not unbearably uncomfortable. The food was excellent in spite of rationing being tightened up at that time. Milk, butter and eggs abounded. The hospital beds we slept on were passable, and bath-water was always hot. There was a choice of magnificent tiled bathrooms; and we were each allotted two bath-times a week. I soon found that very few of our community were interested: some, in fact, maintained that the pregnant should never bathe at all; so my conscience was not strained when I plunged into a soothing hot bath two or three times a day, if time hung heavy.

Only one mother ran away, though a few discharged themselves officially. The runaway mother was continually catching a bus to London; she would then be brought back in a hurry, apparently about to have her baby in the ambulance.

It was surprising, really, how the older ones endured it. Most of them had left their menfolk in London, many in the most dangerous dockland areas. Some had also left children in London. Children over five could be, and indeed usually were, evacuated with their schools. The little ones could only be evacuated with their mothers. Many mothers felt it was their duty to stay in London to look after their husbands, even though it entailed keeping small children in the raids.

The general attitude to maternity at The Barrens was not, therefore, enthusiastic.

"Coo—if I'der guessed I'd fall for one now of all times I wouldn't 'alfer . . . etc, etc," was a not infrequent cry.

Really pregnancy was looked upon as a bit of a disgrace, even by the most heavily married. It made me feel almost ashamed of my whole-hearted pleasure and excitement over the prospect of my own baby. There was only one other mother who already regarded her baby as an important person in her life and not a rather nasty growth.

I had already seen this tall, pretty girl amusing other people's children in an ante-natal clinic queue in London.

I was delighted to find her at The Barrens. Although she was as wide-eyed as I was over the gynaecological witchcraft we heard at mealtimes, Julie was soon ragging me for not taking most of it with a pinch of salt.

There was perpetual speculation about the next to be confined.

"She'll be the next to go, you mark my word," would be said of one barely able to totter. Or, disparagingly, of another, "She won't be gone for weeks. You watch. She'll still be here even after I've gone."

Every mother believed in her heart that she would surprise everybody and "go early", though few did. And every mother cracked jokes about her own personal tardiness, as though we were not all of us dying for ambulances to whisk us away in the night in writhing agony.

Like some religious ritual, each mother as she came down to breakfast glanced quickly round the table in search of empty places. The names of the happily delivered, if any, would soon be supplied, together with full details of the ordeal and such less interesting information as the baby's weight and sex.

A delivery was always stimulating. The turnover was quite noticeable, with an average of forty mothers there at a time. But it was erratic. For a while one or two left daily, then, by some trick of nature, none would leave for a week. At such times every occupant of The Barrens, right down to the man who made up the boiler, wore the pent-up expression of people waiting for something to blow up. Suddenly ten would leave in a night, like hens inciting each other to lay eggs after a thunderstorm. The ambulances would be jostling each other in the drive, for we supplied other hospitals besides the evacuated Westminster at the village of Ripley.

Julie was expecting her baby four days after mine. When I came down to breakfast one morning to find she had gone, mixed emotions of joy and jealousy swept over me. Nobody had heard her details yet, so I telephoned to Ripley. Nothing so far, I learned.

"False alarm, probably," said a well-built young mother called Enid. "Let's pop over by bus and cheer her up."

Popping over by bus was no mean feat, with several changes and long waits; but we achieved it and found Julie in bed, heavy-eyed and speechless.

"They shouldn't have let us in," said Enid in sepulchral tones. "It can't be long now."

A sister passed us carrying a bundle about the size of a normal shopping-bag. Out of it looked the most hideous little face I ever saw on any animal.

"Oh!" said Julie, her face lighting up angelically. "Hallo, James! Aren't you *beautiful*?" She took the bundle and hugged it.

"It's not *your* baby, Julie?" I said in amazement.

"It *is*," she claimed him warmly.

"When was he born?"

"About half an hour ago."

"You must sleep now," the sister told her.

We went away sobered. I had never been so near to birth before. It had the same mystical effect on me as being near death.

"The baby's face!" moaned Enid. "And her so good-looking."

"She thinks he's beautiful," I reminded her. "Perhaps they all look like that to start with." James grew to be a blue-eyed cherub, and then into a little boy who was almost embarrassingly handsome.

Donald came down to see me that day.

"We can't keep a baby in that top-floor flat, you know, darling," he said. News of the heavier-than-ever raids had already reached me.

"There's always the cellar to go to."

"Think of heaving it up and down all those stairs every time a siren sounds."

"But I've planned the flat for a baby. He's got his own little room, and his bath and his frilly cot and everything."

"I know, darling. That's in the flat. Not in the cellar. And things are worse in London."

"Then I must come back."

"Silly."

"I must anyhow if we've got to move."

I insisted on consulting the warden.

"You could go to London for the day, I suppose," she said. "Only take your ambulance-card just in case."

Somebody's aunt offered us a ground-floor flat in Kensington at a reduced rent. We went to see it. It was enormous, heavily Victorian, and slightly damp. It seemed ungracious to turn it down; but, comparing it with our own light, airy, compact little flat high above the trees, I felt this dungeon would be more damaging to the baby than carrying him up and down seven flights of stairs.

Donald agreed about its gloom. He would look for something else. Meanwhile we had better go back to the flat and pack it up.

"All right, darling," I sighed. But when we got there I could not bring myself to touch a thing, except to prepare a wonderful lunch. I had said good-bye to it for ever once before, and afterwards found it quite intact. Now to dismantle it deliberately seemed to be asking for trouble.

"Leave it then, sweet." Donald understood.

A week later he had found an alternative. He asked me to meet him at a suburban station just outside London. My spirits sagged when I saw rows of jerry-built houses with people trotting in and out of them who looked jerry-built too. I found it difficult to show any enthusiasm even over seeing him. But he was in high spirits.

A friend of Molly's had offered to let us her house furnished while she was away on war-work. The rent she asked was so feasible that I felt sure there must be a snag. But there was none. Ten minutes' walk brought us into lanes across a pretty village green. The house we had come to inspect had great charm: it was like a white gabled doll's house, with a neat rose-garden in front and a bigger lawned garden behind. The furniture was good and old and well-polished, and the household equipment was labour-saving and efficient. A part-time gardener and a daily woman were included in the rent.

"It's too good to be true," I said. "There's even a place for the pram."

"You can hang your washing out in the garden," said our hostess-landlady. Yes, between the apple-trees is the place for nappies, I thought, not dripping about the bathroom of a compact London flat.

"Would you like to live here, darling?" Donald asked. We were drinking tea from good china and eating thin bread-and-butter and sugary little cakes. After our *cuppas* and *doorsteps* at The Barrens, I found this soothing.

"I'd love to live here," I said, accepting a home-made biscuit; and as I said it the first wave of mild pain swept through me and I knew that we had started on our next adventure.

9

EVEN THE LAST long climb up the steep drive to The Barrens could not damp my excitement. I had said nothing to Donald about the twinges which came and went as I saw him off at the station. He attributed my happiness entirely to the relief of finding such a delightful house with such excellent amenities for bringing up a baby in war-time. I was happy about that too. Only just in time, I felt, we had been brought literally down to earth from high above Mayfair. I packed my suitcase and went to bed, although I did not expect to stay there long.

At midnight I went down to the kitchen and made some tea. It was the custom at The Barrens for those in labour to do this, usually taking a friend in order to leave someone behind to report details. But I wanted no friend. I had so many exciting things to think about.

There the warden found me, gave me one look, and rushed to the telephone.

"There's plenty of time," I said when she came back, trying to comfort her.

"You never know," she said. "It's five miles to the hospital, and in the black-out—"

She was interrupted by the barking of guns not far from the house. A distant siren piped thinly and was followed by a nearer one. Three bombs dropped in quick succession.

The warden went upstairs to fetch my suitcase.

Presently two very young-looking A.R.P. girls clattered in from the black-out.

"What a night!" said one.

"Where's the patient?" said the other.

"Here," I said, "but there's no special hurry."

"Come along," said one, picking up my suitcase and going out into the dark again. The other took my arm as though I was blind as well as pregnant. The warden said good-bye with an anxious look.

In the back of a car the two girls heaped cushions and hot-water-bottles around me, as though piling sandbags around a public statue. The guns grumbled and yapped; and I became almost hysterical with pleasure that so much seemed to have been laid on for me to remember. It was a brisk moonlit night with just a touch of frost, although it was already May. The girl sitting beside the driver kept turning round to look at me, obviously afraid that I might not last the journey. When the driver lost her way among the confusing little lanes round Ripley, the other started to fumble behind her for a book on first aid. Although it seemed funny at the time, it was really commendable that those girls were not only happy to drive about in the night to the clatter of gunfire and thump of exploding bombs, but were also prepared to deliver a baby, for their country, by moonlight in a country lane, with no guidance except from a book which they had lost.

Their relief was greater than mine when they handed me over to a night-nurse at Ripley Court. For I realised with a giggle of shame that the excitement of the excursion had driven away all suggestions of labour. I felt I ought to go away again. But the night-nurse assured me that all was in order, and started treating me with castor oil and other equally unattractive medicaments.

"If having a baby is worse than this," I thought, "I don't really want to have one after all." I went to sleep.

When I woke up to find myself on an operating-table, surrounded by glass-cases out of which stared shelves full of cold steel, my mind wandered back to the air-raid of the night before, and I wondered where I had been hit. No, of course, I was supposed to be having a baby. But quite obviously I had failed. I got up and stretched, feeling rather stiff from the hard mattress, but otherwise disappointingly well.

The day-nurse I found in the passage, hurrying a bundle to its bath, agreed that it would be all right for me to dress and join the ante-natals downstairs.

In that ward of despondent women I was pleased to recognise many familiar faces including Enid's shining dial. So I was not the only one that had been tricked by a false alarm! Oh yes I was, I soon learned.

"While you was out yesterday, a whole bus-load of us was sent over as suspect. You wasn't even on the list."

So I was the only genuine fraud. I felt terrible about it.

The aimless morning began to drag by; and then, without any warning, a nurse showed Lucy into the ward. It was like some miraculous but undeserved vision, Lucy standing there in the doorway looking so pretty and smart and unwarlike in civilian clothes, when anti-climax had brought me so low.

"It's such a lovely day, I thought we might go for a picnic," she said as calmly as though we were in the middle of a holiday in Andorra.

"Mrs. Anderson is in labour," the nurse said reprovingly.

"If this is labour," I said, "it'll stand a picnic. We needn't go far."

We went into the fields and lay down in the long, lush grass, eating the chicken sandwiches Lucy had brought, and laughing about all the other holidays Lucy had made out of nothing.

"Never before," I said, "have you been so completely lacking in party material." But the night before was forgotten. With Lucy in this mood I could think only of dancing and evening dresses and young men.

A faint twinge reminded me of the purpose of my visit to Ripley. As Lucy left she brought out an extravagantly frivolous pink-and-white chiffon bed jacket.

"Put it on when the baby arrives to complete your joy," she said. It was the most cheering present anyone could have thought of at that moment.

I saw Lucy on to a bus and then wandered back through woods of wild violets, stopping from time to time with an excited certainty that I felt another wisp of pain. But when it had passed I was cynically suspicious once more. I bent down to pick violets for Julie. She was going back to London today. A pain fluttered by, and I knew I should have my baby today. The pain was gone, and I felt desolate and bereaved. I passed a gipsy encampment, with a foal lying on its side and bare-footed children tumbling about their shawled and booted granny. She sat cross-legged, smoking an expensive-smelling cigar.

"Good luck to you!" she called. "A boy it'll be, and born tonight."

"I know," I beamed, for I was suddenly certain again. She asked for no silver and I had none to give. I felt fine and strong and happy, as I had envisaged myself feeling when my day came. Some tanks lumbered past in the lane. I shall remember this day, I thought, with flowers and tanks.

I took the violets up to Julie's ward. She was making up her bed by the window with clean sheets.

"For you," she said and added doubtfully, after looking me up and down, "I hope."

She made up the empty cot too, at the foot of her bed.

"James is charmed to give up his bed to his friend."

Now it was all just fantasy again, a game we had played at The Barrens. And yet Julie had her baby. There might be some truth in it after all. Perhaps in the end I really should have a baby. But now it seemed unlikely again.

We exchanged addresses. I gave our new one for the first time.

She had not been gone long before a pain like rheumatism gripped me across the back. A nurse, seeing me bend over as I walked down a passage, stopped me.

"It's time you had your bath, Mrs. Anderson," she said briskly and ordered Enid, who was much impressed by my progress, to help me fill it.

First we had to light a copper, then carry the water from it into the bath. I was able to laugh until the last bucketful. Then I leaned against the bath and waited for the pain to pass.

"Is it as bad as all that?" Enid asked with a frightened look.

"No. I'm just getting my breath. It's not really bad."

I had promised myself that I should write to Donald once more before the baby was born. I hurried out of the bath, afraid now that I might not otherwise be able to carry out my promise.

I stood by the mantelpiece in the ante-natal ward to write. The other women began to show interest but no sympathy. My case reminded the old hands of other confinements, which they began to describe, but with one eye on me, just in case.

"She ought to keep walking to bring the pains on," said one.

"They don't call them pains no more," said a younger woman, in for her first. "They've worked them out all scientific. They're contractions. They reckon it's silly to call them pains when they don't hurt."

"Aw!" cackled three old mothers of eighteen between them. "Don't they? Just you wait, my girl." They turned back to me. "But she's not getting nothing but niggly little pains yet."

Somehow I managed to screw the lid on the bottle of ink, and to push it and my pen and writing-paper into my suitcase. I had only been able to write a few almost meaningless lines, hurried, as though time was against me. "Glad new house is all right. Glad found my pen. Glad leaves are green and new. Can see a primrose in a potted-meat jar." It would be pointless to try and send it. I struggled towards the door.

"You don't want to go down to the nurses yet," said one of the women.

"Yes I do," I said and went.

It is the practice of midwives in hospitals to appear quite unconcerned about their women in labour, or near to labour, while in fact keeping a doubly watchful eye on them. Consequently ante-natals always have fearful inferiority complexes, though without them, perhaps, they would not so easily become enraged into having their babies just to spite the nurses. I was still an ante-natal and still conscious of my inferiority complex, so I was surprised, when I gave myself up at the labour ward door, to find that elaborate preparations were going on for me.

"I think I really am in labour now," I said meekly.

"Of course you are, dear," I was welcomed by two midwives already wearing masks; and they handed me a clean calico nightgown. "Do the button up at the back until you've had your baby. Then you can do it up in front."

It sounded like getting one's colours for something at school.

"Is that the only way you can tell the difference?" I said facetiously.

"No, dear, it's just a rule of the hospital."

They hurried off to boil up more things in the copper which I had lit for my bath.

They left me alone on the operating-table. I recited the names and ages of my brothers and sisters, the Lord's Prayer, and then the names on the boxes in those wicked-looking glass instrument cases. Anything to keep talking. "Masks. Ripley Court," I read. "Masks and gloves." I repeated these two easy ones again and again. I had no idea how long this would go on. In spite of the table-talk at The Barrens, I had no idea of what to expect beyond a liberal share of Churchill's blood, toil, tears, and sweat.

The midwives came back and took pity on me and taught me how to inhale gas and air from a small machine. At first it seemed to have no effect; but after a while I discovered that, if I could be brave enough to wait until a pain began and then take an enormously deep breath, I could make myself drunk enough to feel the pains without so much actual hurt. The pains were tremendous things now, roaring over my whole body and enveloping it in an iron clutch, and then wearing dully off. I started to work out theories and put them into long and impressive words.

"An excess of unendurability is required to produce the necessary power," I said.

"Does it, dear?" said the sister-midwife with sympathy. "Nurse, I think she's asking for another drink of water."

The party was warming up. Six young men trooped in from playing tennis in the garden. They wore masks and white coats and long white aprons over their tennis flannels.

"Ah, the students," observed the sister.

A young man with dark hair and brown eyes showing over his mask stepped forward and claimed me as his case. From then on he treated me with the loving care and experimental interest usually afforded to a toy engine on Christmas morning. If he could have taken me to pieces to see how I worked he would have done so. The others took notes dictated by a tiny woman doctor, who had floated in unseen and moved about like a ballerina.

The feeling I got now was that we were all in an open boat without oars or sail, in an almost overwhelming storm at sea. As a crew, none of us had the experience of the captain and first mate, but all were able to contribute a kind of cheerful hopefulness to the situation. Whenever, from time to time, I could get my breath I gasped out some fatuous crack, feeling it behoved me, as the central figure, to entertain the company a little.

The duration of these happenings must have been a few hours: yet, if someone had told me it was weeks or minutes, I would have believed equally, so lifted out of time was I.

As the pace grew fiercer, outside interference was added to the drama by the crash of gunfire and drone of aircraft.

"Breathe deeply, breathe deeply," I heard the doctor say. The young men round me started to play jazz instruments.

Oomty-ally-ally, oomty-ally-ally; I floated away from the disgusting scene, but strangely not beyond the sound of distant gunfire, followed by the more deliberate notes of a cuckoo in the garden. Then came a small, high, furious wail above it all; and I was suddenly fully conscious and able to feel something soft and wriggling against my knees.

With absurd appropriateness a far-off air-raid siren sounded the all clear.

"It's a girl," somebody said.

This was an amazing piece of news. We had hardly dared to consider the luxury of a girl. So far there had been nothing but boys among the grandchildren on my side.

I sat up quickly to have a look at this girl. My first impression was of angry clenched fists on a smooth broad chest.

"Well done, old girl," I welcomed her, quite sure that her puckered face was already beautiful.

"Here, we haven't finished yet," the student objected. "Lie down again."

I looked out of the window and saw the white blossom on the pear-tree outside. Funny, I thought, I hadn't noticed it before.

"Time?" one of the students asked for his notes.

"Seven fifty p.m." said another.

Seven fifty p.m. What would Donald be doing? Going home from the Ministry. Not a minute must pass without his knowing about our girl.

"How can I let my husband know?" I asked.

"You can get a friend to send a telegram tomorrow," said sister. "That's the rule of the hospital."

Tomorrow! After all that! He must know now, this minute. Until he knew I could not feel the baby was really ours.

"There," said sister and held the baby up for a moment for me to see. Yes, she was beautiful all right.

Sister whipped a little blanket round her and set her aside out of the way in a cot by the fire. She returned to the foot of the operating-table to finish the job.

I could almost hear sighs of relief now that it was over. The students began to fold up their notebooks; the nurses (and there were several of them now) began to tidy up. I had heard about this relief and joy, but somehow, except in the brief moment when I noticed the pear-blossom, it seemed to escape me. I felt no relief, no joy. I just felt terrible.

The doctor had reached the door. The student whose case I was had picked up the baby to obey sister's instructions and take it to the nursery and wash it.

Suddenly pandemonium broke out, and all was rushing here and there again. I had no idea what had happened, because, whatever it was, it was not within the scope of The Barrens' talks. But clearly something had gone wrong. All sorts of mysterious things were called for, looked for, found by somebody else, and, if they happened to have a sharp point on them, plunged into some part of me. I was too confused by it all to take in what was going on. Nurses must never run except in cases of haemorrhage, I remembered hearing somewhere, yet here they were scuttling around like a lot of rabbits. New and alarming-looking machines appeared; and I seemed to be attached to one by a tube. A report filtered through to my fuddled brain that a cylinder of something had run out.

"We're going to put you to sleep again," the doctor spoke to me directly for the first time. But instead of offering me the rubber mask of the gas-and-air machine, for which I had gained much respect, she poured some nauseous liquid on to what might have been a face flannel and a common sponge-rack, and held it over my face. Disgusting as it was, I breathed deeply. I wanted to get away from it all.

10

THAT NIGHT was known by Londoners as *The Wednesday*. Julie told me she spent it with her mother and her ten-day-old baby cowering under a rocking wall beneath the Coliseum Theatre. It was the worst night of her life. As at a giant Guy Fawkes party, explosions, whistles, and flashes followed one another non-stop all through the night. The damage was enormous, and over a thousand people were killed or seriously injured.

Donald had reached the flat fairly early that evening. There was already that feeling in the air of a heavy raid to come. He ate his supper, ignoring the sirens, and started to pack up our books for the move. At eleven o'clock the telephone rang.

"This is Ripley Court," said a woman's voice.

"Yes?" said Donald urgently.

"We've been trying to get through to you since eight o'clock, but the line must have been damaged. There's—"

"What's the news?" Donald interrupted her.

"Oh, one minute please."

At the Ripley end of the telephone the sister in whose care I had been all day and half the night hurried into the office to find the nurse telephoning.

"She's round," the sister said. "Pulse normal."

"I'm sorry," the nurse said into the telephone. "We needn't have bothered you after all." And then she added as an afterthought, "Oh, you've got a little baby girl."

("She would hardly have been a big grown-up one," was Donald's comment to me when repeating the conversation afterwards.)

"Is my wife all right?" he asked quickly.

"Quite comfortable." This threadbare hospital phrase further irritated Donald, anxious for reassuring facts.

But the line had gone dead.

Comfortable was the last thing I felt at that moment, surfacing in that chamber of horrors, with the nightmare ordeal only just behind me.

My mother would never have allowed this to happen to me, was my first thought. From infancy mothers are there to prevent hurts and ills. This was far too indelicate a business to associate with a husband, and for a while I thought only of my mother.

Then I reflected that my own turn had now come to shelter others from hurts and ills.

A fresh wave of nausea passed through my feeble body. Never again, I groaned to myself. Never again. Donald's and my ideas of a large Victorian family would have to be revised.

The sister came back in a sprightly mood.

"He's got such a nice voice," she said.

"What did he say?" I asked, groping for a glass of water.

"I didn't talk to him. Nurse said it was a nice voice. Oh, I'm so glad you're better!" I really believe she was too: and I felt a little less degenerate for her pleasure. She danced round me after she had taken my temperature, and I almost expected her to kiss me with delight for not being worse.

"And such a dear little baby too," she said. "I'll fetch the students and we'll take you and tuck you down to sleep in the ward."

"Is it too late for tea, Sister?"

"Tea? No, would you like some? I'll ask Nurse to make it, and you can drink it when we get you into bed."

I didn't really want tea, but I had heard at The Barrens that the first cup of tea was the best in a lifetime.

"You don't feel it's properly behind you till you get your tea," they said. I wanted to feel it was properly behind me.

To carry me to the ward, I suppose I expected a trolley to be wheeled in, such as one glimpses in the hospitals of road-accident films. But there was nothing like that at Ripley Court. The lay-out of the house made it impossible. Two students came in and picked me off the operating-table and carried me down and up the steps and along the narrow twisting passages to the bed Julie had made up for me.

My fellow-patients gave me a poor reception. The distant rumbles and bangs had already set their nerves on edge; and, now, being disturbed and getting no details in return gave them something to grumble about.

"Fancy not knowing how many stitches she's had!" a particularly forceful one in the corner complained. "You'd hardly credit it. Oh, Mrs. M.," she called across the ward, "what did you have tonight? They gave me liquid cascara."

A nurse brought me my tea, but it did not have the effect I hoped for.

"I don't know how we're expected to sleep against the clinking of tea-cups," said Mrs. Forceful in the corner, ignoring the rattling of the windows and other much louder by-products of the London raid. "Tea in bed! They gave it to me in the labour ward, same as anybody else. Oo, that cascara!"

The attention I received from the nurses throughout the night piqued them most of all.

"Nobody kept running in and out having a look under my bedclothes," said one. "What d'you think they expect? Twins?"

An outstandingly loud bang, which put the passage light out, had the effect of shooting Mrs. Forceful out of bed and under her locker-flap, where she sat for a while imploring us all to follow suit in the name of the mother of Mary. Nothing could have moved me; and the others preferred to lie in bed and quake. After a while a nurse came in with a candle and shooed Mrs. Forceful back to bed, setting her off again about her liquid cascara.

None of us slept all night. I was haunted by what had gone before. If only I could have brought myself to pour it all out to the ward, the horror would have passed and the others would have been happily employed during the long raid, exchanging their own horrible stories. But I still felt too ill to speak, except to answer the nurses in a slow drawl which I could hardly recognise as my own voice.

"Stuck up," I overheard. "One rule for the rich . . ."

When our wash-basins came at four-thirty a.m. I tried to reach out and dabble my hands in mine.

"Why don't you sit up to it?" said Mrs. Forceful. "Do you good to move about."

The sister, who never seemed to go off duty night or day, swished in and sponged my face and hands.

"H'm," grunted my neighbour when she had gone, "Nobody washed my face nor any other bit of me."

A roar of obscene laughter went up.

Their babies were brought in to be fed.

"Aren't you going to feed yours?" they asked me reproachfully. I shook my head. Surely the old cows knew it was useless to start trying to feed my baby yet? Their memories must be short, for none of them had been delivered many days.

"Poor little mite, letting it starve like that. They're never reared, you know," said Mrs. Forceful, "not them babies what nobody can't take the trouble to bother about."

"Don't you ever stop this bloody awful banter?" I said suddenly.

"Aw!" shocked intakes of breath sucked the room airless for a moment. There was a mumbling of "Never heard such language", "Calls herself a lady", and "Would you credit it?" But from then onwards they were quiet. I was sent to Coventry, in which I sobbed silently to myself, waiting for the day to break and Donald to come.

Beyond the dark blinds a blackbird sang a little fugue. Other birds experimented round it, and then burst into a glad chorus. I thought of my baby and tried to share their mood, but could not. A nurse came in and clicked down the blind so that it shot up in a surprised way, revealing a light sky and a greeny-grey day. There was a mist beyond the old garden wall and a white frost on the ground. From my bed I could see the distant fields where Lucy and I had sat. I lay looking at the new lacy green of a birch-tree.

Hours later, after what seemed like the longest wait in my life, Donald arrived. He came into the ward behind a huge bunch of spring flowers, and passed without embarrassment between the gazes of the night-gowned women in their beds.

My intention had been to make up my face and put on Lucy's pretty bed jacket over a nighty I had made myself (with an eye to cutting it up later into baby's smocks). I had imagined this scene for months. But now I was as stiff as if I had come in from hunting after weeks without exercise. I could not bear even to raise my arm to comb my hair.

I must have looked quite frightful in my hospital night-gown, with the calico-covered button now under my chin and *Labour Ward* embroidered in red across the chest. My face, by nature ruddy, was dead white.

"My God!" exclaimed Donald, when he realised which of the heaped-up women in bed belonged to him, "was it as bad as that?" He kissed me pityingly and turned away.

To my surprise he started looking for the baby. I was not expecting him to show any practical interest in her for years. I was amazed when he began to rootle in the cot at the end of my bed, and then pulled the baby out.

"Hallo, puss!" he said, as a small boy might address a cat with good-humoured affection.

I could hear a clicking of tongues going round the ward over this breach of the rules. Nobody but the nurses was allowed to take the babies out of their cots.

"Let me hold her too," I asked. The babies were bundled tightly in small blankets. Shaped like that, it was easy to understand how they had fitted inside. We unbundled ours and counted her fingers and toes. Her feet were shaped like Donald's and so were her fingernails. But she had the broad cheek-bones of my brother Erroll.

"They've given you the right one," Donald said with seeming relief.

"I'd know if they hadn't. I had a good look at her the minute she was born. She's just the same now, only even more beautiful, and they're all different. I've seen some of the others."

Donald wrapped her up again and put her back. He noticed on the cot-rail the piece of adhesive tape on which I had asked a nurse to write *Marian* above her surname and weight.

"So she *is* Marian!" he exclaimed with pleasure. Marian was one of his mother's names, and, although I had wanted Jennifers and Penelopes and all the other fashionable names strung together, as soon as the baby was born I knew she was Marian—alone.

Donald pulled a chair up to my bed and sat down. "What happened?" he asked.

I told him all about the drive from The Barrens, and the picnic with Lucy, and the violets in the woods. I told him about the gipsy. I stopped my narrative at the filling of the bath with a bucket. The remainder was too crude, too horrible for him. I felt I did not know him well enough to speak of such indelicacies.

We compared notes over the raid in the night. It had been pretty bad in London, he thought. He had noticed a great deal of new damage that morning. People were talking about it in an excited way.

"But weren't you there?"

"Yes, darling. But asleep mostly."

"Not up in the flat?"

"Yes, darling, I was too tired for the cellar."

"How soon can we move to the new house?"

"When you come out of hospital."

"Oh no, please. Move now, as soon as possible."

"All right, sweet. I'll see whether Christine can help." His younger sister was in London on leave from the F.A.N.Y.s, in whose uniform she looked too smart and pretty to move an ink-stand let alone a flatful of furniture.

A nurse came in and asked Donald to see the Sister on the way out. Donald had come all that distance from London to see me, on a journey disjointed by the night's damage. I had lain there longing for him to come. Yet now, after only a few minutes, I wanted him to go. I felt too ill to endure the pleasure of his company for longer.

"See Sister now," I suggested. "Then you can come back and kiss me good-bye."

I lay back exhausted.

When he returned he looked at me with a grave unsmiling countenance.

"Sleep, darling," he said; and almost before he was out of sight I had drifted into sleep.

When I woke up later in the day I was surprised to see my mother sweep into the ward. She wore diamonds with her W.V.S. uniform, the jersey of which she had knitted herself of angora wool. She carried flowers and fruit and cream and soft pillows for my head and soft blankets for the baby. She greeted all the patients as warmly as she greeted me, admired all the babies equally, and divided the flowers among us.

"You ought to have had your baby at the rectory with the district nurse," my mother said. "She's quite used to these sorts of complications. Everybody in the village has them. They've fitted out her bicycle now so that she can perform almost any operation to do with having a baby herself."

The memory of the dreadful things the doctor, midwives, and six students had done to me without the aid of a fitted-out bicycle came back to me. On the whole I felt that perhaps I was better off at Ripley.

Donald must have sent for my mother, and she was pleased. She offered to fetch me in her car when I was ready to leave the hospital, and drive Marian and me to the new house.

She managed to catch up with the same whirlwind that seemed to have swept her in, and swept out with it.

The other mothers drew themselves more apart from me than ever. But they had to admit, in whispers among themselves, that I was a curiosity, what with my language and my mother's diamonds and the extra medical attention I was getting. "Some sort of show folk," I heard muttered darkly.

Only when they overheard a corpulent man in a navy-blue suit lecturing to the students over my prostrate form did they change their tune.

"It's her wound, see," said Mrs. Forceful after the little procession had moved on. "Had to have it done like my sister's friend. I thought she looked bad when they brought her in, poor thing."

"Delirious, she was. Didn't know who she were."

"That's all them blood transgressions. How d'you feel now, Mrs. A?" they all asked me warmly.

Basking in reflected glory, they now claimed me as the pride of the ward. Better than that, they could boast of me more fluently than I could myself, until I had learnt the jargon.

"Once," said my neighbour, unable to resist taking some of the kudos from the others, "I lay in next to a centurion."

"Still, a wound can be a nasty thing too," said Mrs. Forceful.

Later I learned that wombs are wounds the world over wherever the English language prevails.

It was good to be on friendly terms with my fellows: but a week went by before I felt anything approaching joy and relief. All the possible minor difficulties liable to crop up after a first baby seemed to afflict me. Feeding the baby brought agonies; but I was assured that successful feeding would help to put everything else right.

"Come along," an attractive young nurse addressed my baby, as she handed her to me to feed, "make mummy better."

I burst into tears of self-pity.

"What's the matter?" the nurse asked in surprise.

"Just the idea of her making me better," I sniffed, "when she's so young."

It took me a few days to love Marian passionately as my own. At first I loved her as I love all babies, because she was charming; then she snuggled into my heart and settled down for life.

I began to think about our new house and to make plans for giving it personality as our home. Most of our furniture had to go into store: and Christine was dealing efficiently with that.

All the baby-equipment and some of our own had gone to the doll's house.

In making any plans at that time, there was always an alternative that had to be kept in view. At any moment might come a fork in the road. One way would lead on for me to the doll's house, lined with quiet domesticity, looking after the baby and Donald, when he got back from London each evening. The other, which could not be ignored and had to be kept in good repair, led to the possible invasion by the Germans. No plans could be made for the first without making due allowance for the second.

I longed to be able to rear my baby in comparative peace and comfort. On the other hand I could not help being infected by Donald's enthusiasm for a chance, particularly strong after a successful Home Guard exercise, to come to grips with the enemy. He did not wish to see his country invaded; but his imagination could not but be stimulated by Churchill's "We shall fight on the beaches, we shall fight on the landing grounds, we shall fight in the fields and in the streets, we shall never surrender." I too was stimulated, even though I knew that I should get no more than a worm's eye view of the excitement—with fright, anxiety, and a lot of agonising boredom, waiting, hunger, and discomfort; and others, if not ourselves, might suffer miserably. No, the thrill of hearing the church-bells ringing the invasion alarm, like the thrill of hearing the first siren, would not be worth it, even though I was convinced that we should defeat the enemy if they came.

All the same, I was glad of that spark of excitement. Without it, contemplation of that second road would be too grim. I told myself to make the most of the restful period that had come my way and get strong for emergencies.

Donald had worked out a route by which I could take the baby, on foot if necessary, to the hills of Wales, where we had friends ready to receive us, working in the secret "skeleton" armament factories. He intended giving me his pistol for my defence, leaving himself with only a sword, for the Home Guard were still pathetically short of modern weapons. He would have to stay with his battalion in London and experience the painful difficulty he had told me his men often had in deciding whether their duty lay with him, in defence of their important building, or with their families, protecting them and helping them to escape into the country.

The strain of that decision, plus his very hard work, showed in a new photograph of him that stood on the locker by my bed, but it could not eclipse his look of distinction and charm.

After a week Enid joined me in the next bed. Her husband, now in the R.A.F., came to visit her on the day her baby was born. He looked acutely embarrassed by her description of her confinement, which she had already unburdened herself of once in the ward. Searching for any unobstetric diversion, he turned his attention to Donald's photograph.

"Hallo," he said, "I know that man. He used to walk through my beat when I was a park-keeper in Green Park."

At that moment Donald appeared in the ward. Both fathers greeted each other like old friends meeting unexpectedly in the jungle. Donald's visit to me that day had to be short, because Enid's husband could not wait to rush him off to the local to get his baby behind him.

11

THE NEW PRAM swayed gently on the grass between borders of summer flowers. The promised row of clean white nappies fluttered in the wind among the apple-trees. Christine had moved us perfectly, and stayed on to settle me in. My mother had driven us to our doll's house from the hospital, Marian wearing handmade clothes for the first time, and a ridiculously large woollen bonnet. The house was easy to run; the baby routine, according to the handbook, was going well. I should have been content.

But I was not. I still felt ill and looked it.

"People always feel whacked after a first baby," somebody told me. "It's largely psychological, you know. Anti-climax and all that."

I pushed on. The routine was a full one; but now I started to work on a big christening party. Our wedding had been unconventional: our christening must make up for it. Our two families had not yet met and mingled. I sent out invitations, and was flattered that many of the relations were prepared to come a long way to the party, some of them agreeing to stay with us over the week-end.

Donald's mother made an exquisite christening robe of beautifully-joined antique lace. I made a big cake from carefully saved rations, but could not quite muster the strength to ice it (with the last two pounds of icing-sugar we were to see for years). I'll feel stronger in a day or two, I thought. Then I can do it.

About a week before the christening, Julie came to see us from London with her baby. *The Wednesday* had shaken her badly. *The Saturday* had driven her back into the country.

"We're evacuated on a ghastly woman," she said. "I'm only allowed into the kitchen to cook twice a day, and I have to do James's washing in cold water."

"Stay the week-end with us," I suggested, "and we'll find something better round here. It would be fun to be in the same village."

"Lovely," said Julie. "I never see another baby to speak to. We could meet with our prams and queue for cornflakes together."

Julie came and we started to look for a billet for her. But nobody wanted evacuees with babies. They cried at night, they used too much hot water, their washing hanging in the garden attracted enemy raiders. Babies seemed to have every kind of vice. "We'll find a place in time," I said.

"I must find somewhere before tomorrow," said Julie. "You seem to have forgotten that all your relations are coming to stay."

I had not forgotten. I just felt so appalled by the prospect of giving a party that I preferred not to think about it.

"Never mind about that," I said. "Why don't you stay on with us? Be our evacuees. We could have fun with the two babies."

"What? You bag the Government's eleven bob a week?" Julie teased me. "No, we can't stay here."

"And you can't go back to London tomorrow."

"I'll see about it," said Julie.

I went away and lay on my bed. I felt terrible. When Donald came home from London he took my temperature. It was high enough to alarm him into sending for a doctor, although it was nine o'clock in the evening.

A Scotsman arrived. Within half an hour I was being carried out of the house on a stretcher with my baby beside me. Julie brought my suitcase. The sight of the ambulance was making her cry.

"Ambulances always do," she sniffed, "and fire-engines."

"You can't leave here now," I ragged her. "You'll have to stay to run the christening."

"Anyway, I could look after the house," she said, "and Donald."

But she did run the christening. It was too late to put off the guests. Donald's mother had started her journey to us. Julie iced the cake, the first in her life, and got in food for the party. She made up the beds, with a mattress for herself and James in the air-raid shelter.

On the day of the christening she turned up at the hospital where I lay, feverish and fretting. She brought with her the robe of antique lace in which she dressed Marian up, so that I could see her in all her finery. She stuck a sprig of London Pride in her wisp of golden hair, and carried her away wrapped in a Shetland shawl I had been keeping for this day.

My mother brought Marian back after the service. Pinned to the baby's dress was a diamond pendant I had often seen my mother wearing.

"A christening present for my first grand-daughter," said my mother, "but for you to wear, darling, till she's grown-up."

On the lawn at home, James was standing in for Marian. While Julie helped Donald to entertain the guests, Donald's mother, deprived of her newest grandchild, pushed James's pram up and down on the grass, and talked to him in the baby language she had revived from her memory for Marian.

"Never rock your perambulator," she warned Donald. "It joggles the child's brains and loosens the nuts of the pram."

*　*　*　*　*

As a connoisseur of hospitals, I could tell in five minutes that the one I was now in was bad. It was inefficient, and the treatment ordered by the doctor was not carried out.

In the surgical ward across the passage, I could see blood seeping through the patients' bandages and being left to drip on their sheets. I was in a private ward, where I was even more neglected, except by the matron who had obviously set my room aside as being a good place to exercise her golden retriever in wet weather. She had hair like his, except that it was less muddy. They would come in together for a romp two or three times a day, and then she would turn to me and pass on any news she had.

"Got a woman in the next ward," she said. "Came in just like you in the night. Just had her baby. Opened her up. Full of pus. Nothing to be done. Just had to shut her up again. She's dead now."

I insisted on going home long before I was well. A few more days in that place, and I should have joined the woman in the next ward.

As it was, I was no better at home, and soon considerably worse.

"How did you find this new drug M and B693 affected you in hospital?" asked the Scotsman.

"They never gave it to me."

The Scotsman swore and produced a bottle of the pills.

"Then you shall have it now."

M and B, in its early form, brought on a frightful depression, nausea, and the general effects of a choppy Channel-crossing. Certain foods had to be avoided. All this was bearable; but I was no better and in fairly considerable pain.

A nurse was imported who had once laid out a duke's aunt. There was nothing she could not—and did not—tell me about the behaviour of the nobility, both before and after rigor mortis sets in. Her patients usually died and she was not expecting me to be any different.

Julie's sister came to look after the nurse. My mother came to see what was happening. Donald had a difficult time sorting all these women out and, at the same time, falling in with any little whims I might have. A London specialist was sent for; and the corpulent man in the navy-blue suit who had lectured over me turned up.

"Can't tell with these puerperal infections," he said, pocketing his cheque. "Better get her into the county hospital where they can do some blood-tests."

"And the baby?" Donald asked.

"Leave that here."

"But I'm feeding her," I said.

"You're not now," said the specialist and departed.

A few minutes later Julie brought the baby into my room, where the nurse was sulking over the thought of somebody else laying me out.

"I shall buy Marian a bottle," said Julie. "It's perfectly simple. I've seen it done. You just mix up a lot of powder and stuff together. It doesn't smell very nice but the baby'll drink it."

And so Julie added looking after my baby to looking after my house and my husband—as well as her own baby.

"Well! We shan't need this again," said the nurse with finality, shutting my make-up case, which we had never needed anyway since she came, into my top drawer.

Vaguely aware of the drama of the situation she was making, I decided to add to it by asking Julie to cut off all my hair. As a child I had wept over a Victorian novel about a little musician who, in a high fever, had all his beautiful curls cut off just before he died. Julie had never cut hair before and was not particularly keen to start now. But it sounded so like a last wish, that she agreed "to have a clump at it": and clump it off she did, every curl and wave of it. It was never the same again, which served me right. She had everything against her—inexperience, blunt scissors, and an ambulance drawing nearer, ringing its bell all the way up our road.

It was a heavy old thing, of the sort usually given only to F.A.N.Y.s to drive. I was heaved in on a stretcher which fitted on to steel runners. My mother decided to come the twenty miles to the hospital with me, for which I was soon grateful.

The driver belted along with tremendous fervour, ringing his electric bell in short unmusical bursts of urgency as he swerved round other vehicles, on whichever side of them came handiest. Every time we rattled down a hill my stretcher slid with a thud against the front partition. Every time we roared up a hill, my mother only saved me from crashing out of the back doors by hanging on to them with all her strength.

She tried to stop the driver, but when she beat on the panel, he only kept his finger more firmly pressed on the bell-push and drove faster, presumably supposing she was urging him on to reach the hospital more quickly. Between her attempts to stop him, she had to scramble to the back of the ambulance to hang on to the doors before we went uphill again.

After the driver had rammed on both brakes in a stop-skid outside the hospital, so that I shot forward like a human cannon-ball, he admitted to my mother that he had never driven an ambulance before.

"Normally," he said, "I drive a fire-engine."

I was put into a glass-walled cubicle in the fever block. But it was very different from my first fever block in the midlands. The nurses came in so often to see whether I wanted anything that sometimes I shut my eyes and feigned sleep just so as to go on resting.

The young gynaecologist who took over my case visited me frequently and had tests made, but suspended all medical treatment. He told me afterwards it was just a matter of sheer wait and see. If he had had banana leaves and a hut in the tropics, he would have wrapped me in them and laid me in the shade to die.

Donald came often, although it was an awful trek by train and bus and on foot. At first I was too ill to speak to him, and it seemed such a waste of his time and energy. Then the fever subsided, and I was too weak to speak to him. It was wonderful not to feel actively ill, but I had never known weakness before, and I think it was my complete dependence on the nurses that angered me back to normal.

They were a cheerful, noisy lot. They took great trouble trying to get me able to eat again. Friends and relations sent eggs and other delicacies which were impossible to buy; but I could not fancy any of them. The young gynaecologist ordered a pint of stout at every meal. From that day my strength began to return and I could eat again. In a few days I could sit up, and within three weeks of my coming to the hospital I was demanding to feed my baby again. I knew I was being a bad bargain to my family, and felt that the least I could do was to try to give Marian again what the textbook called her *birthright*. It was the textbook that gave me the idea. Mothers had been known to produce milk after anything up to three weeks' separation from their babies.

The gynaecologist was amused by my suggestion. He was a debonair young bachelor who had been heard to complain of his lying-in mothers that they made no more use of their bosoms than if they were clothes pegs. He thought the experiment with my baby worth trying and likely to do me good.

When Donald had satisfied himself that there was no danger in letting Marian into that area of infections of one kind and another, he brought her along in her carrycot to share my isolation and help to entertain the nurses. She was already pretty and friendly and was in every way a delight to me.

Assisted by various stimulating drugs, I was soon the medical marvel, feeding Marian successfully and pleased to have some purpose again. We spent five more weeks in the hospital; but the weather was good and French windows opened on to a garden so, with Marian to play with and books to read, the time of segregation passed not unpleasantly.

In due course we went home. My clothes, cut for a normally rounded figure, hung on me in loose folds. My wedding ring fell off if I put my hand down, so I had to tie a piece of rag round it to keep it on. I was not well all that summer, but with Julie beside me I muddled through the ordinary routine of a wartime house-wife. Our two babies were well matched. James was already beautiful. Both had blue eyes and were very fair. At about the same time they sprouted golden curls. Often we dressed them alike and pushed them out in the same pram. They played about on a rug together in the garden while Julie and I ate our standard lunch beside them, lettuce from the garden and tapioca pudding made with our extra rations of milk allowed because of our babies.

I saw very little of Donald. He left by an early train for London and came back late, or, if he was on Home Guard duty, not till the following night. On Sundays he was so tired he slept half the day. Our biggest excursions together were wheeling the pram through a nearby wood. But I could not complain. Few of my friends saw their husbands for months at a time, some not for years, some never again.

The worse the war news became, the harder Donald's department had to work to counteract its effects on the minds of the world, without distorting the true picture. The Germans had failed in their attack on our morale with indiscriminate bombing of urban areas. Their air effort slackened. But they had been successful in North Africa, Greece, and Crete; and now their advance into Russia made heart-breaking news, as night after night we heard over the radio new names of Russian towns taken by the German army.

The fear of invasion in this country was no less. Donald's ambition for his Home Guard was that, if the Germans got as far as London, he would make the Ministry of Information the last building to fall. He would then tell the survivors of his garrison to crawl in ones or twos through the surrounding enemy, to take up the fight somewhere else. He himself (still immortal) would fight a sort of one-man rear-guard retreat towards Wales. Meanwhile he persuaded Julie and me to make a nightly habit of packing the prams with food and clothing for our journey to Wales.

"Couldn't we stay here and polish off a few of the enemy ourselves?" suggested Julie. On the whole we felt we should be as likely to survive if we did, as we should be after a two-hundred-mile walk into Wales.

"If you're really game to do it," Donald conceded thoughtfully, "the best method might be to fill the house with Huns, then start a fire in the cupboard under the stairs. It'd work easiest if you made them tight first."

"What on?" Julie and I linked our little fingers.

Autumn came, and I went quietly back to the county hospital for another long session. The attacks of fever and pain continued into the winter after I returned home.

Bad news became more personal. Donald's mother, charming, witty, and always to the point, had escaped from the Germans in Guernsey. When I became ill again, she came to our rescue and helped Julie to nurse me at home. She was eighty-three, but her energy was boundless and on our behalf she worked herself tragically to death.

A fortnight before Christmas, the Pearl Harbour attack by the Japanese was followed next day by their sinking of H.M.S. *Prince of Wales* and H.M.S. *Repulse*. Two of our greatest friends were in those ships. Dick survived and wrote me an illustrated letter describing his experience vividly, and his thoughts as he waited in the water to be rescued, watching his ship go down against a brilliant sunset. Then he was lost in the fall of Singapore. His young widow, who had only known a few weeks of marriage, pined and died. Meanwhile we waited for months for Alec, our other great friend, to turn up; but he never did. He was Marian's godfather. Her other godfather, my young cousin Hugh was to be killed three years later in a skirmish behind the enemy's lines.

It was a grim, sad, long winter. When I saw an almond-tree in blossom and heard a thrush sing, I was ashamed to look and listen. There was no place for spring.

Lorema became engaged to a young naval doctor; and those of the family who could escape from their duties congregated in Hampstead for the wedding. It was smart to be shabby, and we all were: except Lorema, who wore such a dramatic blue-veiled hat that the *Evening Standard* kept her on the front page of all its editions, in spite of an avalanche "somewhere in England".

Soon Julie's and my babies were a year old, and we asked some children to tea. But without biscuits and sugared buns and an iced birthday cake it was not a party. No crackers, no paper hats, no balloons, no ices to end up with. Children who had known all these things had no compensations for being moved out of their homes, as many of them had been. At least our babies expected no treats, except lease-lend orange-juice and government cod-liver—and other fish—oil.

Now I went into a London hospital for an operation. My first caller was Julie's husband, Malcolm, whom I had never met before. It was exciting to meet him, but I knew that he would now take Julie and James away from us, as he would be stationed in London. Life without them in the doll's house was difficult to imagine.

The surgeon at the hospital made no promises of a cure.

"There are two more possibilities," he said "Hysterectomy—removal of the womb—and pregnancy."

"I'll try the second," I said.

"After all this it may take you five years."

It did not take us five years. Just over nine months later I was being admitted to another evacuated maternity hospital nearer home. This time everything went smoothly. The house was less picturesque but more practical. The labour ward was a cosy room in which a coal fire burned with a contented flutter.

My first view of Rachel was of what looked like a pink rabbit being held upside down by its feet. I should have known that yell anywhere as belonging to my family.

Donald was with me within an hour. I had been moved (by trolley) into a room with French windows which opened on to a lawn running down to the river, beside Hampton Court Palace. I was sitting up in bed, full of all the joy and relief I had heard so much about.

Donald was amazed so see me looking so well.

"So there's nothing to it nowadays, if all goes according to the book?" he said.

"Oh yes there is," I assured him. Now I knew him well enough to give him a fairly graphic confinement story. He bore it well.

He went off with a nurse to look at the baby and came back to report that she was pretty, golden-haired, and had small feet. The nurse had told him she was a very small baby.

"Let's call her Rachel after your mother," he said. I was already privately calling her Rachel, and delighting in the fact that we had another girl. The nighty I made for Marian's birth was all ready to cut up into two girls' frocks.

Donald telephoned the news to my mother and told her we wanted to call the baby Rachel after her. My mother, like other exceptionally generous people, is a bad accepter of gifts or honours.

"I see," she dismissed it quickly. "Now, Donald, please tell Verily that I've darned up all Marian's socks, and I'm now starting on her vests." Marian was staying with her.

Donald came back to tell me he was afraid we had offended her.

"Oh no," I assured him. "At this moment she's probably tearing round the village telling everyone, 'It's a girl and they're calling her Rachel after *me*'." She was too.

The hospital was Jewish and so was the food, which was excellent. Cleanliness also came higher on the list of essentials than in most hospitals I had met. I ate cake and drank wine at the circumcision feast of the baby in the next cot. The men of the family stood, wearing their hats, round the mother's screened bed while she fed the baby, which I found a touching part of the ceremony.

It was strange that in the nursery of rows and rows of newborn babies, nearly all with dark hair and skins, there were Pamelas and Violets and Rosemarys and Richards and Stuarts, but only one Old Testament Rachel.

We took Rachel home, and Marian was brought back to meet her. Marian was nearly two, delightful, monosyllabic, and self-willed. She was shy or resentful towards me after our fortnight's parting; but she romped with Donald and twiddled his eyeglass on its string. We let her discover the baby in its cradle herself; and perhaps that contributed towards the admiring affection she has always had for Rachel. In the course of rollicking round the room, she came to the cradle and stood up on her toes for the routine inspection she had been giving it for months. She gave a cry of delight when she found it filled, and dragged up a chair and climbed on it to get a better view. Then she leaned over in an effort to heave Rachel out in her arms.

We sat Marian down on the floor and put the baby across her knees. She cuddled her with a safe carelessness that she has never lost when harbouring babies or young animals. Notorious screamers become docile when gathered up into Marian's school satchel, just as though they were a natural part of her homework.

With two babies I was always busy, but I was well, and this was a new enough sensation to rejoice in. This time I was present at the christening, which is more than can be said for anything much to eat or drink. However, Norrie, now in artillery uniform, produced a bottle of port; and Lorema, pouring it out (it must be admitted, near the kitchen sink), cunningly managed to make it go round the forty loving friends and relations who turned up.

Marian had already learned to fill the gaps at a party with home-made entertainment. It was a warm sunny day, and now she took off the clothes I had spent so much time washing and frilling for her, invited the younger guests to undress too, and then turned the garden-hose on them. It was a great success.

"What a mercy," observed Norrie who had not been blind to the desecration of his port, "water's not rationed yet."

Our ship seemed to have sailed into still waters, but not for long. Overwork, lack of sleep, snatched and inadequate meals, rushing for trains, and anxiety over the war and my illness had their effect on Donald. He started to have asthma.

He would wake up in the night gasping for breath; and nothing I could do relieved an attack, which only increased in frightfulness as the night wore on. I tried making him hot drinks, opening the windows, shutting them, producing pungent smoke from a lighted cone I had seen advertised as "instantly relieving", offering him ice, lighting a fire. But only time seemed to have any effect.

It was hard to believe that such distress could not cause severe damage, if not complete collapse. It was harder still to have to sit patiently and wait for the spasm to pass. Once an attack began to abate only at dawn and Donald fell into an exhausted sleep.

I hated having to wake him early, especially since it was Sunday, but he was due to go off to address a meeting in Leicester Square. He was to speak of the value of women learning how to shoot. Perhaps Julie's anxiety to have a slosh at the enemy encouraged him. But his painful journey had its reward. As a result of his speech, the notorious Lord Haw-Haw announced over the German radio that Donald's name was on the blacklist of British war criminals. What could be more brutal and internationally unfair than to incite British women to defend themselves and their homes against honour-loving soldiers of the Reich?

"I don't suppose I shall ever win a higher award," Donald said.

A few days after the Leicester Square meeting, Donald failed to turn up at his expected hour. Usually, if he was delayed, he telephoned: but tonight no message came. I spent an hour or so in looking out of the window, listening for the sound of his step on the gravel, making an extra-special salad for his supper to welcome him, and walking a little way along the road, certain I should see him coming towards me round every corner. Then, wife-like, I let my mood change and allowed my mind to linger on an exceptionally intelligent, cultivated, and very chic woman, whose appearance became clearer and clearer in my imagination the more I thought about her.

Drinking a cocktail beside her, in perhaps the opulence of the Dorchester, was Donald. How easy to step in there after the high-level meeting they had attended together! How simple to graduate from discussing the outstanding points on the agenda to alluding to the colour of her dark, clever eyes! Had he not had to put his arm about her shoulder when he taught her how to hold a rifle during his first mixed Home Guard meeting?

She could wear her expensively-cut skirt as tight as that with her figure. She could get away with jewels in a war-time hat. Her stockings were from New York, and her degree from Oxford. With anguish I admitted she was everything I was not. But how false she was at heart! How could Donald be so deceived? I withdrew the salad from the supper table, and ate it myself.

The telephone seemed to follow me about the room in a black silent way, so that I could not avoid looking at it: but it refused to ring.

I went upstairs to draw our bedroom curtains. And suddenly the woman became blurred; and I was seized with suspicions of something worse. Could Donald have shot himself while teaching her and her companions how to shoot? Or could he—more likely—have been overcome by asthma on his way home? What if he had an attack in the blackout? He would be unable to move or shout for help? Now I started to make a really hot soup to welcome him.

The telephone rang at last. I tried to answer it calmly.

"Hallo, sweetheart," Donald said in a jaunty mood. So it was that despicable woman!

"When are you coming home?" I asked weakly.

"I'm going to try and catch the last train from Waterloo," he answered affably.

"Who've you been with?" I had to ask.

"Oh—er—well."

"What was she wearing?" I pushed on grimly.

I could hear Donald laugh.

"A blue siren suit," he said.

"I suppose you're going to tell me you've been drinking with Winston Churchill," I said with haughty sarcasm.

"I'm not going to tell you anything till I see you," Donald said, but quite sweetly. "Don't wait up, darling."

"I shan't," I said and put the receiver down and went to bed.

* * * * *

During breakfast, the Prime Minister's drinking companion wandered in unshaven and looking short of sleep. He bent down to kiss me.

"Well, who was it?" I asked ungraciously.

"You were right," he smiled, "the P.M."

"You mean you went to Downing Street?" I said, considerably less coldly.

"No, Chequers."

"But why didn't you tell me on the telephone?" I said excitedly.

"'Careless talk costs lives', darling," Donald reproved me.

"But anybody can go and look at Chequers and see if he's at home, can't they? It must be easy enough to tell."

"Oh no, it isn't. The house and grounds are wrapped in secrecy. Barbed wire and long weeds and six-foot guardsmen with machine-guns in the laurels. I was only told he wanted to see me at once, and to go to a car at a certain spot in London and get in and wait and see. There was no time to telephone you. I'm sorry about that."

"But what was it all about?"

"Well, we've had a flap on for the last few days over some missing newsreel film that was shot somewhere the Boche haven't occupied yet. We thought it must have been hi-jacked by the enemy. We've sometimes snaffled his. It would have been bad, because it hadn't been censored. Finally we found it in Scotland, held up by snow. Meanwhile the old boy took an interest in the excitement, and set his heart on a particular piece of music to be put on the finished film. I didn't want him to have it."

"What a shame, if he'd set his heart on it," I said warmly. "Poor old man!"

"As a matter of fact he was looking remarkably youthful. His voice in real life sounds much younger than on the air. Anyway, the censorship point was that the music he wanted would have given away that the place is garrisoned by American troops." Donald was the chief official film censor. "I only discovered it was a famous American regimental march late this afternoon. I'd been trying to get hold of it, because the P.M. wanted it, but found there wasn't a single sheet of music of it in the country, and no bandmaster had ever heard of it. I tried everywhere—even Malcolm Sargent."

"Did that satisfy the P.M.?"

"Not a bit. He said I was wrong. *He* possessed a record of it. 'Then, sir, you've got the only one in England,' I said. 'It's a splendid tune,' he said. You know how pro-American he is. He went over to his gramophone cup board and produced it. It was just the stuff for a barrel organ. He marched up and down the carpet like a happy corporal."

"Did he give you a drink?" I asked eagerly.

"Oh yes. The Canadian Prime Minister was there. I'd met him before. Mary Churchill's very pretty. I sat next to her on a sofa."

"I suppose you're going to teach her to shoot?" I said, trying to drag myself away from the voice of excited curiosity, back to the lofty tone I had been preparing for him through the night. But I couldn't help adding, "What did it all look like?"

"I wish we lived there. Comfortable, mellow, and plenty of personal treasures. And nice people. Any hot water for a bath?" Donald got up and stretched. "I spent the night on Waterloo Station, taking turns with a naval stoker to lie down on the only unoccupied bench."

"Oh, darling!" I said anxiously. "Without a coat? Here, have my coffee—I've only just poured it out—while I go and get the bathroom ready for you."

* * * * *

On a night not long afterwards Donald again did not appear at his accustomed time, nor telephone. It's only the Prime Minister again, I told myself confidently. At eleven o'clock a knock on the front door made me look to my black-out. A knock at this time usually meant that an air-raid warden had spotted a slit of light. Donald, of course, would let himself in with his key. I went to the door and opened it to a stranger with a car.

He had picked Donald up at the station, where exhaustion had brought on one of his near-strangulation attacks. Together we got him into a chair and I telephoned a nearby doctor. He came at once and injected adrenalin. Donald slumped, suddenly pale and relaxed. He remained in the chair all night. At first I kept coming down to look at him. After a while I brought my eiderdown and sat in the chair opposite him until the baby woke for her first feed.

After that the handsome young doctor would come along our lane with his pyjama jacket tucked into his trousers whenever I telephoned him in the night. Then we bought a hypodermic syringe, and he taught me how to inject Donald so that I could nip a severe attack in the bud.

The first time I did it, my hand shook so much I could hardly fill the syringe. It is bad enough to have to plunge a sharp point into anybody who is not an enemy. But when Donald blanched, sighed, and lay still I was sure for a moment that I had injected him mortally with an air-bubble.

We saw specialists. Donald was tested and found to be allergic only to horses. There were no horses left to cut out of his life, except a milk horse which he rarely saw nearer than the end of the road. Nevertheless, unwilling to disbelieve in the magic of Harley Street, we threw good money after bad on expensive and useless courses of treatment.

"Can't we try something drastic?" I suggested. "I never got better until we did."

"I don't think having another baby would cure me," said Donald.

"I don't mean having another baby. I mean something else. Moving back to London, for instance. That would cut down travelling and rushing for trains. Perhaps the air doesn't suit you here too."

Only for love, I thought, would I say this. We were happy there in the doll's house with the two little girls. I was just beginning to enjoy it.

"What about bombing?"

"No bombs have dropped on London to speak of for nearly two years." I found myself twisting my wedding ring, an unconscious trick I had when trying to exert my will over myself. I was trying to make myself want Donald to agree. I had faith in the idea that he might be better in London. But we had the summer before us. The lupins were out again.

"All right, darling," said Donald. "I'll start finding out about houses."

"Or a flat," I suggested, thinking of housework, "with a garden."

12

FOR A LOW RENT we were offered a pleasant family house in St. John's Wood, with a good garden. Some bomb damage had just been repaired, and the owner was not anxious to have the house requisitioned with its new windows and clean paint and walls.

It was not a flat and it was not small, but it was friendly; and with my natural optimism I hoped it might not be much more difficult to run than the doll's house. True, the basement kitchens covered a big area; and the sink, in the scullery, was a good twenty paces from the gas cooker. The kitchen stairs were long and steep and winding, but there was a service lift up to the dining-room. It struck me as ingenious till I tried turning its heavy handle.

Only one other house in the road was inhabited. Behind us a long crescent of over a hundred huge empty villas was slowly disintegrating, with the aid of the weather and former bombing. It was an eerie street to go along, with some of its ornate houses lying flat in their own gardens. Rotting laths and powdered plaster mingled with the mud along the untended roadway.

The furniture we took out of store was enough only for a small flat, and now we had a four-storied ten-roomed house to fill. But in the deserted gardens of the crescent I had seen broken chairs and tables and bedsteads. If the shops were empty, I knew where to get what we needed.

The blitz had played some queer tricks with its victims. Into our garden had been blown a broken lawn-sprinkler, which we converted into a standard-lamp for our drawing-room. Beside it lay a linen-basket which we bent back into shape and painted a nice shade of crimson and cream. From other gardens, sometimes digging a little to unearth them, I collected curtain-rods and rings and coat-hooks and other things needed, but impossible to buy then, for moving into a new house. Donald was too law-abiding to relish this pilfering as I did, but he ceased grumbling when we had got our loot safely into the house. And he took an attractive pleasure in restoring it to a usable state.

A nursery fire-guard was something impossible to find in any shop. The day I stepped out of a bombed site with one in my arms, I walked straight into a policeman. I thought instantly of the notices saying that looters might be shot. The policeman shook his head in a disappointed way, as though he expected better of me.

"I know," I said. "I'm ready. You can shoot me."

"It's not that, miss," he said. "I've had my eye on it to take home after dark for my own toddler."

"Take it," I said, holding it out to him. I knew now what thieves meant by *hot*.

"No, miss," he said sadly. "You got it first." And he continued on his beat.

Soon we had collected enough furniture to be able to take in a lodger, which the greater expense of living in London in a big house made necessary. A really beautiful young French aristocrat, whose husband had been gaoled for political deviation, brought her baby son to live with us. Our attraction for her was probably that ours was one of the few houses in London with a children's nurse, or so she thought from having seen a uniformed figure pushing a pram out of our gate towards the Zoo; for Our Annie, who was not yet fourteen, was proud to dress up like the real thing.

But, on the very day Germaine arrived with her little Ton-Ton, Our Annie's mother came up from the country and reminded me that big boys, as well as baby ones, were not outside Our Annie's scope.

"Choir-boys in a country lane's one thing," she said, packing her daughter's bag for her, "but when I see all them American soldiers loafing about the streets of London, I says to myself— it's another."

Ton-Ton fitted between our girls in age, and also in the pram. When it rained, I pushed them all up to one end under the hood, where they would fall asleep interlocked like a litter of puppies.

Germaine had a lot of friends in London and liked going out. With three babies in the house, I looked for a replacement of Our Annie.

The best offer came from a young woman who had recently been dancing in the chorus of the Windmill Theatre. She had somewhat mysteriously just come out of hospital. We asked no questions, and engaged her for a small wage in consideration of short working hours. She was to begin work late each day, after breakfast in bed, and knock off after tea at five. I fixed up a few comforts in her room for her long evening rests; but I need not have bothered.

By day she was a drab little thing in a pale overall, whom Germaine, and eventually all of us, addressed as "Nanny". But regularly at six o'clock she would descend from her room in all her lustre and step out into the night.

"It's her other job," Germaine observed when, one evening, she was having supper with us.

Donald raised his eyebrows.

"Photography," said Germaine. "She's a model."

"Mm," said Donald, "she's not bad looking when she's made up."

"Perhaps," said Germaine. "But you'd never think she'd wear a fishing-net for work, would you?"

As soon as we had got the house looking more like a civilised home and less like a battered encampment, our minds turned towards giving a party. There were a good many of our friends within reach whom we had not been able to see for a long time. The drink situation was still difficult, but in London slightly more possible. Nanny put on my going-away dress and Germaine wore my only evening dress that I had not cut up into chair-covers. This left me with my pre-war Sunday dress. Germaine looked adorable and all our friends were enchanted and intrigued; but I was sorry to see she had cut the bottom off my dress instead of turning it up. I had been saving it for after the war.

Norrie was on leave from his anti-tank battery, which he secretly loved but complained about to cover his adoration.

"What's the point of coming back to London?" he said of our move. "It's the worst place for asthma. Everybody knows that. Besides, nobody has children in London now. It's far too much of a responsibility." Norrie always goes on like that.

"But still," said Beryl, whose gentle charm was not by one stitch disguised under the thick navy-blue uniform she wore as an able-bodied Wren, "it's lovely to have Verily in London again, for when you can get leave."

Norrie refused to be side-tracked. "What can you do with children in a raid?" he asked aggressively.

"There hasn't been a raid for two years." Even as I said it the old, once-familiar upward swoop of a siren came through the chatter of party voices. Another siren and another and another and soon all were howling together. It was not much of a raid. Just enough to change the subject. What was later called "the little blitz" had begun.

After the party Nanny went out as usual.

Sometimes she only came home in time for breakfast; and then I tactfully went back upstairs and pretended I had overslept until she was safely in.

On one occasion, after another raid, she failed to turn up even for breakfast. Donald had gone to his office. I felt I should give her the benefit of the doubt and telephoned the police. Yes, there had been a number of incidents during the raid. The names of the victims had not yet been circulated. I gave Nanny's name and a description of her. Then I started to bath the babies.

A few minutes later the telephone rang. It was the police station I had telephoned before. Would I care to step along to identify a body similar to that of the aforesaid young person?

"No, I wouldn't," I said quickly, and then felt remorseful. Outside it was cold and foggy. Nanny had nobody else but us—so she said. "All right," I said, "I'll come."

I fed the baby and gave Ton-Ton a crust to be going on with and went into Germaine's room, where she was still asleep.

"Just going off to identify Nanny's body," I said.

"I don't suppose anybody's ever done that to it before," Germaine said sleepily.

"Be an angel and watch my babies," I said.

As I reached the front door the telephone rang. It was a hospital in Seven Sisters Road telling me that Nanny's body was with them, unconscious but with definite life in it.

"Can you come and fetch her?" I was asked.

"Unconscious?"

"She'll be all right by the time you get here."

"Is it as far away as all that?"

I was given some directions, which sounded simple enough. But it was hours before I reached the Seven Sisters Road.

At the hospital I was taken straight into the casualty department. There was Nanny, stretched out on a couch, still drunk enough to call me "Honey Pie".

The nurses were as anxious as I was to get her away. One offered to get a taxi. I accepted the offer, and between us we helped Nanny into it.

"It washa fall," she said, "a tremendoush fall. All the way down the Piccadilly escalator."

I was perfectly willing to accept the statement; but, to prove it, Nanny insisted on our going to the Westminster Hospital.

"They know me there. They'll undershtand," she said. "It washa fall," she repeated, "a tremendoush fall. Not a fight," she added confidentially.

Besides watching the taximeter ticking up, I was also thinking of Germaine and the three babies, and wondering whether she had grown tired of guarding them and, if so, where she had gone to.

The casualty department at the Westminster Hospital seemed to know Nanny well enough not to feel any need to X-ray her.

"Take two aspirins," the student who examined her said earnestly, "and sleep it off. It's the only way."

We found another taxi to carry us home. Germaine was still there, but only just. She was already late for a lunch appointment.

"I would have taken Ton-Ton with me but as I'm so late—be an angel and feed him." As she passed she took the tortoiseshell comb out of my hair and swept her own dark hair up into it. "You don't mind, do you? It's such a nice one."

I put Nanny to bed first with the two aspirins, then set about the three babies. They were none of them hungry, so no doubt Free French chocolates had had to be distributed liberally as bribes throughout the morning.

At six o'clock Nanny skipped down the stairs, bright and spry, her hair waved and scented and her face made up to look like a milkmaid's.

"Ta, ta," she waved as she clip-clopped on her high heels out of the front door.

The telephone rang.

"It's Germaine. I'm held up. Be an angel and put Ton-Ton to bed. Has he had his tea?"

"Yes."

"And his supper?"

"Yes."

I knew I should have to pay for that morning in the Seven Sisters Road.

The sirens began to wail as I rang off. I had no idea where Germaine had telephoned from. This was the first time I had been alone with the babies during an alert. I wondered whether I ought to move them downstairs or not.

The local guns cracked out loudly from Ordnance Hill. There were more and bigger guns in London than when we last lived there. They sent me tearing up to Ton-Ton's room which was on the top floor. I pulled him out of his cot and ran down with him to our babies' nursery. I pulled Marian out of her cot and set her on her feet. She merely folded up in a sleepy ball on the floor. I put Ton-Ton back under one arm and picked Marian up under the other. Now, how could I carry Rachel down? I could not. That was the answer.

I put the other two on the floor while I dragged Rachel's cradle away from the window. Then I carried the others down to the drawing-room and dumped them there while I ran up to fetch Rachel. Another burst of gunfire made me jump the last four stairs and swing round the bannisters with one arm while I clutched Rachel in her shawl with the other. Now that I had them all in the drawing-room it did not seem enough. I must do more. I seized a table and put it on its side between them and the window. I roofed it with an oil painting from the wall.

Donald strolled in from the office with his brief-case, as I was about to climb into the compound with the babies.

"Hallo, darling. Nice game?" he asked us cheerfully.

All my panic left me. I stood up rather sheepishly. The gunfire was really nothing, only an occasional clatter. There were no bombs falling anywhere near us.

"I think I've had a harassing day," I said.

We talked by the fire for a little. I fetched Ton-Ton's supper and, long before the all-clear sounded, we carried the babies back to their cots.

But from then onwards I decided to put Ton-Ton's cot in our bedroom when his mother was out. I knew now that, if I really had to get the babies down in a hurry, cutting out that extra flight of stairs would make all the difference.

Next day I told Germaine that I intended to sack Nanny. One reason was that when I wanted her most, in the evenings, she was out.

"Nanny's all right," said Germaine. "Why don't you go out more yourself? You stick in here and get stale. Nanny likes a good time, but who doesn't? You should be more broad-minded about Nanny."

"I could hardly be broader," I said, thinking of the Seven Sisters Road again.

"You do too many dull things. Babies, cooking, washing! It gets your ideas all out of proportion. Other people don't worry about air-raids."

"Other people don't have the lives of three babies in their hands."

"But I would have—gladly. Any night you like. Or, if you don't want to leave them with me, Nanny'll stay in while you two go out and enjoy yourselves. Listen," Germaine became enthusiastic, "tomorrow night we'll all go to the Bagatelle. First we'll meet at the French Club. You and Donald and a sweet Frenchman called Achille. And me."

"Honestly," I began, "I don't want to go out. I like it at home."

"You can't like it. It's just you're in a rut."

"If there's a blitz I'll want to rush home."

"There won't be a blitz."

There was no blitz. But the evening was a hundred-per-cent flop. Although Germaine and Nanny had taken great pains all day to beautify me so that I should be unrecognisable when we met Achille and Donald, I had no heart for the outing.

"Good Lord!" said Donald when he saw me, putting up his eye-glass. "Nanny's false lashes!"

Those were almost the only words he spoke. To the thud, thud, of the dance-band we drank champagne at the Bagatelle. To our tired eyes the hangings looked tatty and the people behaved foolishly. We were both too sapped by the war and work and the babies to do more than sit and wilt until the time was decent to go home.

"Funny," said Germaine next day, "I expected you'd both be such good company."

One night a baby whimpered and I opened my door to go to her. Coming down the stairs was the shadow of what might have been an American sailor.

After breakfast I sacked Nanny. There was quite an ugly scene, made uglier by Germaine's imploring me to take back my words.

"You'll regret it," Germaine said. "You won't be able to manage without her. Nannies don't grow on trees, you know."

I knew that, but I felt this nanny had gone too far. She left with a clatter, and Germaine hurried out to a lunch appointment.

Germaine came back at midnight. Dancing had made her prettier than ever. Donald had just come in from Home Guard and we were drinking tea by the drawing-room fire.

"Ton-Ton still in the garden?" Donald asked Germaine cheerfully.

"Why should he be?"

"Because that's where you left him when you went out."

"Oh my God!" exclaimed Germaine, foolishly rushing towards the garden door. "Did I forget to ask you to bring him in and give him his lunch? I'd forgotten you'd thrown Nanny out."

"Don't be silly," I said. "Of course I fed him. He's been asleep in his cot for hours."

"You've been complaining to Donald then," she accused me. Of course I had.

"Now I'm going to complain," said Donald. "Why don't you look after your baby?"

"Verily loves babies. I don't."

Donald was suddenly roused into one of his rare rages.

"You come here and eat what little food there is in the country, sleep all day, dance all night, shirk your own responsibility. What use d'you think you are being to the allied war effort?" he stormed.

"The war has a broad back," Germaine shrugged her shoulders as only pretty Frenchwomen can.

This taunt was more than an overworked government propagandist could allow. Donald finished his tea, put his cup down, and then asked her to sit. With all the subtlety of his wartime trade, he laid the situation out before her. He gave her facts and rhetoric.

Germaine listened, and a big tear blobbed on to her skirt.

Next day she got herself a job with the Free French. But her husband's politics were against her. For a few days she was watched. In the black-out a small Free Frenchman hung about in our bushes by the front door. Her job ended. She got another job in an English food-shop, where politics were of no account.

With Germaine keeping regular hours and leaving the house when Donald did, after breakfast, I found I could somehow get through the day with the three babies without any help. It was the hardest work I had ever known, and I had to run to keep up with the daily programme. But it was rewarding.

Marian was enchanted by Ton-Ton, who was just beginning to totter with uncertain steps and bursts of merriment. On sunny days she mothered him in the garden, occasionally abandoning him for some private game of her own. She liked jumping for a barrage balloon. Maybe these good-natured-looking elephants seemed near enough to her to reach, some hundred feet or so above the garden. Or perhaps her inherited optimism made her believe that she could raise her own stout form that much from the ground. Rachel lay and cooed in her pram until it was time to bundle the other two in with her to go and do the shopping. Not that there was much to buy in the shops. I was lucky if I managed to bring home so much as a pound of carrots over and above the rations. By Christmas week the shops had been stripped, but I had saved enough food to make a meal which was, at any rate, different from the usual dried-egg omelette.

By Boxing Day a cold had dragged me down to a state of morose grumbling. Ton-Ton too had a cold. He coughed and the mischief went out of him. For a little while Germaine cosseted him in the French manner with mustard-plasters and footbaths. Then she grew bored.

"Be an angel and watch him," she said, removing the necklace from my neck and fastening it round her own. "You don't mind, do you? It goes so well with my black suit."

"No," said Donald unexpectedly. "Verily's going to bed."

"Then I will gladly look after all three," said Germaine, shooing them into the drawing-room.

When I came down later, Donald was alone with the three babies. Marian and Ton-Ton had piled everything in the room within their reach on to him where he lay, in his chair, too tired to restrain them.

"Where's Germaine?" I asked.

"Just gone to fix up about some party this evening. She won't be long."

"Now who's letting themselves be bossed about?" I said, gathering up the babies for tea. Germaine was right. I loved looking after Ton-Ton. He was a darling. After tea I worked on his cough with a steam-kettle and stayed with him until he slept without coughing. But I was late for Rachel's feed and she was yelling. I blamed myself for having that rest on my bed. It put me behind schedule.

Next morning Germaine surprised me by bundling Ton-Ton into his pram, although it was still foggy and his cough was not much better. She tipped such clothes as I had washed and dried for him on to the top of him and wheeled him away.

When she came back without him I was anxious.

"What've you done with him?" I asked.

"He's ill," she said shortly. "I took him to a French doctor."

"Is he in hospital?"

"No, the doctor has recommended a nursery home where he'll be properly looked after."

I ought to have been relieved, but instead was furious. Ton-Ton being dumped on strangers when he was feeling ill! Germaine suggesting that I neglected him! It was more than I could bear.

"Then I won't have you in the house either," I suddenly burst into a storm of rage. "Get out!"

Germaine turned and looked at me with an amused but quite affectionate expression.

"You want the world," she said. "You want my baby and you want me to look after him on my special Boxing Day holiday. You want everything your own way." She went upstairs and packed. She came down with her suitcases. She had ordered a taxi by telephone.

"Good-bye," she said. "And you know where to find me when you feel sweet again."

I thought I should never feel sweet again. But next day the house seemed dead without her. Even asleep, or out at a party, she contributed something lively and gay to its atmosphere. I rang her up at her shop and apologised.

Ton-Ton was better. Now Donald had the cold. He went on going to his office until the week-end, and then became unusually pale and silent.

Rachel was teething and woke me more than once in the night. My own cold was still stuffy. When woken at six o'clock in the morning, I felt cross and ready for a long sleep. I asked Donald to bring me Rachel. Something in the way he lifted her from her cot made me order him back into bed. He sat there without asthma, but looking so hot it was obvious he had a high temperature. I cursed quietly to myself and went to get the thermometer. I took it out of its case and dropped it in the wash-basin. The mercury chased round the rim of the plug-hole, and slithered down the drain.

"Well, do you *feel* ill?" I asked Donald irritably, as though he had complained.

He nodded; and something about his lips made me start to dress. It was Sunday morning and too early to telephone a doctor, with nothing to offer in the way of symptoms except an intuition that my husband was very ill. I planned, as soon as it was light, to borrow a thermometer from the only other inhabited house in our street. There lived an Admiral with his friendly wife, who had once trained as a nurse. As soon as I saw her pull back her curtains I went over to her.

Mrs. Vivian lent me her thermometer and came back with me to see Donald. I took his temperature. It was 106°.

13

"YOU TELEPHONE the doctor," said Mrs. Vivian, "while I go and collect my belongings. Your husband's going to need a good bit of nursing, and you'll need help."

When the doctor came he diagnosed lobar pneumonia. It was before the days of penicillin, and the life of the patient still depended on the skill of the nurse. It was the greatest relief to me to know Donald was in Mrs. Vivian's professional hands. I am not a natural nurse, and the severity of the illness filled me with such terror I hardly dared go into the room where Donald lay. I moved my things into the nursery.

For two days and nights Mrs. Vivian hardly left Donald for more than ten minutes at a time. A lung specialist was brought in and only increased my fear. "We hope to pull him through," he said in a much too calming voice, patting my arm. Until then there had never been any suggestion, as far as I was concerned, that we should not. The illness itself frightened me: now came the added fear of what it might lead to. Frantically I tried not to widow myself in my mind; but it was uphill work, because Donald looked desperately ill and each hour he became worse rather than better.

The babies still had to be fed and washed and cared for. I applied myself to them with increased fervour.

Mrs. Vivian, with almost no sleep for two nights, was reeling on her feet. It took two nurses to replace her.

One was a stout elderly day-nurse. The other was a pretty but more starchy night-nurse who went home to sleep by day.

The day-nurse found Donald an impossible patient, chiefly because, like Churchill who had pneumonia soon afterwards, he objected to being washed. The night-nurse found him enchanting. He no longer seemed to belong to me, so I took no part in their discussions.

Any illusions I had ever had about the romance of nursing one's dear one through the valley of the shadow of death were shattered. The whole ghastly week had a cold horror about it which had no bearing on the Donald I knew. I found the whole thing much more harrowing than my own serious illness two summers before.

The first sign I noticed of Donald's recovery was a slight return of asthma. It was a relief to hear some familiar sound come from that awe-inspiringly quiet room.

Donald asked for a glass of beer. This was heartening news. The doctor, who had not known us before, left a message with the day-nurse about four whiskies a day. It reached me as a prescription that he must have, four times a day. Whisky was probably one of the most difficult liquors to find in London. But I set about finding the four a day, which I mostly had to buy by the glass. For two days Donald drank them unwillingly, and then wrinkled his nose and signed to me to drink the next one. He still wanted his glass of beer.

I consulted the doctor. Of course he could have beer if he wanted it. What he meant was that he should not have more than four whiskies a day.

The raids began again. It was no use making the drawing-room, or safer still the lift-shaft, our shelter, because Donald could not be moved. The only thing to do was to persuade myself and others that his room on the first floor with a big bow window was the only safe place in the house, and to congregate there.

Although some of the raids were quite shaking, they had little effect on me. I was sure that the suspense I had just endured had cured me of ever being afraid of anything again.

The day-nurse always joined us in her dressing-gown, and sat bolt upright in a chair with her face tilted upwards like a hungry hen. The night-nurse busied herself brightly making tea. Rachel slept or cooed in her carry-cot. Marian bounced about the floor, trying to get a glimpse of what was going on through the black-out curtain. To please her we put out the lights and let her see the arcs of fire in the sky as the guns fired. When a bomb whistled down, Marian threw herself giggling on to Donald's bed, saying,

"One two three and a—"

"Bang!" she shouted with delight as the bomb exploded.

"More bangs?" she asked hopefully.

"Oh, the woos," she said regretfully of the all-clear, knowing it meant that she must return to bed.

As soon as Donald was well enough to talk, he asked for his assistant at the Ministry to be allowed to see him. At first the doctor said no, then, realising that worrying over his work would do Donald more harm than the actual work would, he allowed her to come.

Cokie and I had often exchanged messages over the telephone. And years afterwards she told me what kind of a wife she imagined I must be from my voice and from Donald's way of addressing me.

"Tall, svelte, and very smart," she said, "very much in the fashionable set. I came to your house simply terrified, and climbed up all those front-door steps and rang the bell. Suddenly a tousled head popped out from the basement, and what looked like a schoolgirl, with bare feet, shouted to me to come down. I asked if Mrs. Anderson was in." When I said I was Mrs. Anderson, Cokie claims I could have knocked her down with a feather bed.

Cokie and I got on well together. Her healthy lack of respect for Donald was a helpful antidote to my present intense veneration of what had so nearly been the dead.

"Isn't the old sod up yet?" she said. "What? Still lying about like a railway-line?"

Even the day-nurse, who reluctantly let her into Donald's room, failed to quell Cokie. She settled down to sprawl across his bed with her files and papers spread round her. I was surprised to come in and find him sitting up expounding a plan with his old verve, for all his weak appearance and voice.

It was a relief to be able to part with nurses and to cease to feel an outsider in my own home. Moreover they were costing us almost as much as Donald earned.

Lucy and her parachutist husband turned up and offered to stay the night and look after Rachel, while I took Donald down to Sussex for a change of scene. It was a generous offer, because they had a baby of their own at home and Michael rarely got leave.

I took Donald to the little inn where we had spent our honeymoon. I settled him into bed in the room we had shared before, and took Marian on to my mother. Marian loved staying with my parents and they seemed to welcome grandchildren at any time.

I went back to Donald in the inn. He was sitting up in bed with a rug round his shoulders, looking pale and thin. I had a longer look at the room. It was just the same and probably had not changed much in the past five hundred years. There were notches in the beams which I remembered exactly from our honeymoon. Last time I looked at them I had been looking forward. Now I looked back.

"Being married to you's much better than I expected it would be," I said.

"Good God!" exclaimed Donald. "What could you have imagined worse than this?"

"Sloping walls and children under foot getting on our nerves, and us bickering. I've seen it all happen to the nicest people."

"Then what foolish whim allowed you to marry me?"

"I knew it would be worth it whatever happened. But even if a few walls do slope in our attic, we've got masses of straight ones, and the children are a joy, and you never seem to want to quarrel."

"Thank you, darling. If you're happy then I am—intensely."

How tired he looked! Was he really fit to be left alone tomorrow?

"I know," I said suddenly, "stout! Wonderful stuff!" I went down to the bar where we had sat on our wedding night, and ordered a glass of stout.

Next day I went back to London. Michael had gone. Lucy handed over the baby and left too. I wrote out an advertisement for a single lodger and posted it to *The Times*. Then I set about clearing up the house after the turmoil of the nurses. The last people who lived there had had four maids. We had none. Never mind—with nobody there but the baby and me, progress was noticeable.

By bedtime the house was fairly presentable; but its emptiness lessened its attraction. I went up early and pulled the carry-cot over beside my bed. I turned out the light and lay down. Something creaked in the nursery. I put the blankets over my head and then remembered Marian's kitten, Choopy, which she had brought in one day from a deserted garden.

I got out of bed and went into the nursery, but could not turn on the light because I had not drawn the blackout curtains.

Something brushed against me. Was it the kitten? Yes, it was soft and furry. I carried him into my room and shut the door.

The creaking went on.

I steeled myself to go back. Outside on the stairs, the house seemed enormous. Old houses always creak, I told myself. It's something to do with the shrinking boards.

I was not very convinced, but the thought helped. I looked out of the window and saw the outline of the roofs of all the empty houses stretching away into the darkness. There was no comfort in them. The baby, the kitten and I were cut off in a creaking world of our own.

The night passed slowly. It was years since I had been afraid to put my light out. What would happen if the baby woke? Should I ever have the courage to go down to the basement kitchen to warm milk for her? I lay awake, sweating with fear of nothing.

Suddenly a familiar sound broke the tension. Outside, the air-raid sirens were beginning to soar and plunge through the air with their wailing notes. Happily I gathered up the carry-cot, put the kitten on the end of it, and trotted down to the kitchen. With the guns booming outside, I felt among friends. A bomb exploding dispelled all further suggestions of the supernatural. We three settled down contentedly in the lift-shaft.

A week later I fetched Donald and Marian from the country.

Donald pottered about the house, but was still weak and pale and easily tired. Every night the bombers came.

Marian became so used to them that, before I could reach the nursery when a siren sounded, she had climbed sleepily out of her cot and was trying, in the dark, to heave Rachel out of hers. One night I came up from the kitchen to find her at the top of the stairs in her pink pyjamas, with her blobby gold curls over her face and the baby bundled up in a shawl in her tubby arms. I picked them both up together and carried them down to the lift-shaft where we now always sat with Donald and Choopy in a raid. Marian liked to sit on her high-chair with an apple.

Donald and I sat on the floor with the carry-cot and the kitten between us.

It felt safe enough, with no windows and two walls between us and any exploding bombs. And then, one night, the little grocer's shop where we bought our rations had a direct hit. The father, mother, and little girl always sheltered in a cupboard under the stairs. They were buried. All my theories changed. One must be able to get out.

"Sweetheart, it really makes no difference," Donald tried to assure me. "None of these old houses are designed as air-raid shelters, but they give better protection than being out in the street. All we can do is to take reasonable precautions and put ourselves in the hands of God."

But many broken nights had driven me beyond reasonable precautions. I moved our camp out of the lift-shaft and into a small basement-room with a window, against which I loosely piled furniture. For Marian I made up a bed on a shelf in a cupboard, and put mattresses on the floor for us.

There was no raid that night. We slept soundly upstairs.

14

MY ADVERTISEMENT for a lodger appeared in *The Times*. There were two answers. One was from a single girl called Marjory Crow. The other was from a man who followed up his letter with a telephone call. He had a pleasant voice, and I agreed to meet him to discuss the possibility of his lodging with us. I put on my West End suit and made up my face and left the two babies sleeping in Donald's charge. A single man, bachelor or grass-widower, was exactly what we needed. He would be undemanding and his friends would ask him out to dinner.

"Why the wedding hat?" Donald asked.

"We must impress him."

"Don't overdo it."

I came back hardly able to face Donald.

"Well," he asked "is he coming?"

"Yes."

"You don't sound very happy about it. What's he like?"

"Oh, charming, very attractive," I hastened to assure him.

"But—?"

"Well, you see, he's got a wife and four children."

"That's all right. He'll have to go home and see them quite often."

"He can't. They're all coming too."

"Darling, is that really necessary?" Donald asked in alarm.

"He was so awfully nice about us and they've had a ghastly time. One of the children's terribly delicate and another's a bit queer apparently."

"And who looks after these four children?"

"The wife, and she'll help with ours. We're going to share the cooking and housework and they'll share all our expenses."

"It sounds a rotten idea."

"We can't let them down. They've nowhere else to go."

Donald said nothing else until supper-time.

"I've put your friends off," he said.

I made a little fuss but it was an enormous relief.

A few mornings later I noticed their names in *The Times* as bankrupts.

"With shared expenses," said Donald, "that might have been good-bye to all our furniture."

"Perhaps with shared expenses," I said, "they might not have gone bankrupt."

"Good Lord," said Donald, taking the paper from me. "It's old Bertie. I've known him for years. Poor old Bertie."

"Ought we to have them then, after all?" I asked nervously.

"Not on your life—not old Bertie! He's been sharing houses with the wives of chaps in the club for years. He used to be a member. Many a happy home has been laid waste by old Bertie and his crew."

"So either way we should have lost the furniture?"

"Rather! Darling, I must go."

Donald was going to the office for the first time after his illness. It was bitterly cold.

I washed and ironed dresses to take the babies out to tea in. It gave me a bad conscience when there was so much essential housework to do. But Marian hardly ever went further than the shops and Rachel had never been out to tea.

When we got there, Marian discovered and consumed half a pound of chocolates, one person's sweet-ration for six weeks. I left embarrassed, with Marian unrepentant and Rachel whimpering with tiredness and the cold. Snow was falling and it was rush-hour and the buses were full. I stood on the edge of the pavement with Rachel in my arms and Marian walking maddeningly round me hanging on to the hem of my coat. We were no attraction to the few taxis that ambled past looking for American soldiers who would pay double fare and take them to the remunerative West End. We would not go out to tea again till after the war, I decided.

The lowering sky promised heavier snow. The atmosphere was threatening and promised an early air-raid. At last a taxi took pity on us; but the sirens sounded just before we got home and the miserable driver made me pay double for exposing him to danger. There was no danger yet, but I could not keep the babies out in the snow to argue with him, so paid him and then regretted it.

Instead of putting the babies to bed in their cots, I put them on the shelves in the basement, and immediately this small damp room assumed a magical quality of safety for me.

Donald came in exhausted, hoping for a comfortable period of recovery in his fireside chair, to find me refusing to allow any of us to leave my damp little dungeon. He sat on the edge of a mattress while I darted into the kitchen to warm up a meal for him. It was one of those long silent alerts. Marian, excited by the tea party and by the novelty of her shelf, could not or would not sleep. Donald felt too tired to undress.

"But you can't go to bed in your clothes," I objected.

"You can't go to bed on a store-cupboard floor," he countered, lying down on his mattress and shutting his eyes.

The all-clear sounded.

"Shall we go up?" I suggested.

"If you like." It was midnight and none of us except Rachel had been to sleep yet. I started to gather up the babies and some of the bedding. Donald came slowly up behind us.

Halfway up the stairs the sirens began again.

"Shall we go down?" I asked.

"If you like."

"We'd better," I said.

"No!" said Marian, crossly. "Want to go to bed. Want an apple. Want a potty." Suddenly she was sick. I was so busy dealing with her that I hardly noticed the clangour of raiders and gunfire which broke out above and around us.

We went back to my shelter-room, and I pushed Rachel in her carry-cot under the table and put Marian back on her cupboard shelf. I had to break my security drill and go upstairs to fetch clean clothes and bedding for Marian. On my way up I could see through an unblacked-out window that the garden was like a firework display. Incendiary bombs spluttered silver fire about the frozen grass. Upstairs I could hear them bouncing off the roof. Normally Donald would have loved to be out on the lawn dealing with them.

I ran up to the attic to make sure none had penetrated the roof. So far we were lucky. I fetched the clothes and went back to the basement, where Marian was being sick again. I dealt with this and then cuddled her down. "One, two, three, and a—" she said unhappily, as a bomb whistled down. "Bang," she almost whispered.

It was the noisiest night since the old blitz days.

Once more Marian was sick, and I had to go up for another lot of clean clothes and bedding. Part of the garden fence was on fire but it was some way from the house. We should have to leave it. A bomb whistled down as I went back to the others. As in Tom Tiddler's Ground, I nipped back to safety. Marian had scrambled out of her cupboard to reach the asylum of Donald's knee before the bang. "One, two, three, and a—" she was still shouting breathlessly. She refused to go back to her shelf. "One, two, three, and a—" she said again, standing up and holding on to her pyjama-trousers with one hand, as we heard another bomb fall. And then, instead of her usual "Bang" when it exploded, she opened her mouth and screamed. I felt my nerve snap too.

But trying to comfort Marian helped to blanket my desire to scream as well. I held her in my arms and she buried her face against mine with each crash. I looked up to see that Donald had taken the baby out of the carry-cot and was holding her away from the window.

My barrier of furniture fell down as the house shuddered with the crump of a nearby bomb. The glass shattered inwards. We leant over the babies with our backs to the now open window as another bomb came down and another. We could hear a plane dive just above us. The guns clattered out, shaking the house again. Marian made no sound now. Further away, six bombs dropped one after another. Then everything was quiet.

Presently the all-clear sounded.

"This place isn't safe," I said, rather obviously. "We must go somewhere better."

"All right, darling," said Donald soothingly. "Let's move into the lift-shaft if they come again." I could see he was all for going up to bed immediately.

"Nowhere's safe in this house."

"The Vivians have got a shelter in their coal-cellar."

"That's not safe either."

"Where d'you think we should go?"

"Into the Underground station."

"But, sweetheart, it's half a mile away! They might come again before we got there."

"I know, but once we were there we should be safe. Or at any rate we should have done the best we could."

"All right," said Donald, "if you feel that's the best."

We carried the babies up to the hall, and I pulled out two prams and put a baby in each.

"Can't they both go in the same pram?" Donald asked, pulling on his overcoat.

"No, Marian was sick. It might not have been the chocolate. Perhaps she's getting a cold, and the baby might catch it."

Donald smiled. "Mustn't risk catching a cold on a night like this," he said.

He pushed one pram and I pushed the other, with the black kitten held firmly in my free arm. Marian was chirpy now and enjoying the adventure. Donald kicked a smouldering incendiary across the street and it went off like a roman candle. The pavement outside our gate had been pitted by them.

At the end of our street, rescue workers and wardens were clearing up an "incident". The steady hacking sound of their tools mingled with occasional orders or demands made in low voices. An ambulance stood by. A lone plane droned over and my feet took control. I reached St. John's Wood Underground Station with the small pram, pushing it in through the door, and then senselessly ran back to Donald and the big one.

Inside the circular entrance to the station, lights glowed and quietness soothed. The escalators were stationary. We left the prams at the top and walked down, carrying the babies and hiding the kitten in their shawls, in case animals were not allowed in public shelters.

On the platform regular shelterers slept on steel and wire-netting bunks. The shelter warden allotted us two bunks. Donald stretched himself out beside the baby, and they went to sleep at once. Marian and I tossed around on our wire-netting, to the roar of the air-conditioning appliance which drowned all sounds from above.

"Where's the choo-choo?" Marian wanted to know. But we must have fallen asleep just before the first train rattled through the station at about six. I could hear it only in my dreams. From then onwards they ran every ten minutes, disturbing sleep like a recurring cough.

The shelterers began to stir, gather up their blankets and carry them away. The escalator, working now, took us to the upper air. A warden at the top gave the welcome information that all was clear.

I was still jittery when we had breakfast.

"The fact is," I said, "I'm terrified. I never used to mind as much as this."

"It is terrifying," Donald agreed, "seeing Marian frightened. She showed last night that all this time she's been pulling our legs. I don't believe she's ever enjoyed the raids as much as she seemed to. She was just making light of bombs dropping, like you do. But it can't be doing her any good. I don't think she should be in another raid."

"Nor should any of us," I said with feeling.

"I have to stay in London. But I think you three ought to get out. It may not be for long. After all, it's the Government's policy to evacuate mothers and babies."

"Where shall we go?"

"To your parents?"

"What about you? You're not really well enough to be left yet."

"I'll stay at the club."

"Will you promise to go down to the shelter when other people do?"

"Yes, when other people do."

He went off to the office and I started to pack up a pram with all we should want for a week or two away from home.

The front-door bell rang. A pretty girl stood on the doorstep.

"I'm Marjory Crow," she explained. "I answered your advertisement of a room."

"Come in," I said; and suddenly an idea came to me. "Where's your job?"

"I haven't got a job exactly, yet."

"D'you want a job—with the room, I mean?"

"What is it?"

I explained that I could not keep the babies in London any longer; but that my husband had not yet recovered sufficiently from pneumonia to fend for himself. Could she cook his breakfast and buy his rations?

"Yes, I think I could," she said. She was really very pretty, fair, eager, and blue-eyed with just that innocent wistfulness that men find attractive. Ah well.

"I say, is that your typewriter?" she asked irrelevantly.

"It's my husband's."

"D'you think he'd let me borrow it?"

"If you came here. Yes, I'm sure he would."

"No, now. You see I've got the chance of a marvellous job, only everything depends on typing part of it quickly, and I haven't a typewriter."

"Do it now," I said, "while I pack."

She sat down at the dining-room table and laboriously picked out the letters.

While I packed I wondered whether it would really be wise to leave her there. For one thing, would she be capable of cooking breakfast? I rather doubted it.

"Cooee!" she called. "I've done it."

I went down to the dining-room.

"My typing's not very good. D'you think it's all right?"

She showed me a list of measurements in yards.

"Whatever is it?" I tried to sound interested.

"It's a piece of land. An awfully nice man gave me the job. A friend of a friend of a friend's. You know how you meet people like that these days," she rambled on. "He took me down to the

Isle of Wight to take the measurements. His firm's thinking of buying the land after the war for making an airfield."

"An airfield?" I repeated.

"Yes. Now I have to give the measurements to *another* man I've never met," she giggled. "Isn't it complicated?"

"It sounds like fifth columnists to me," I said.

"Oh, no? D'you think so?" Her blue eyes rolled with surprise at my suggestion.

"I wouldn't give the measurements to anybody except the police," I said.

"Oh no," she said. "They'd only laugh at me. Besides, I'm being paid to help. I'm sure it's all right. I don't see why they shouldn't want a new airfield in the Isle of Wight."

"Don't you see?" I said, almost becoming abusive over her stupidity. "You're just being taken for a ride. What you're doing is not only dangerous to you, but to the country."

"Oh, I'm sure you're mistaken. I must fly now. I'll get in touch with your husband about the room, and cooking breakfast."

She tripped down the steps with the typewritten list.

I tried to telephone Donald. He was at a meeting. I told Cokie about Marjory Crow.

"Yes, dear, I know," she surprised me by answering. "Your husband's been telling me all about it."

"But he doesn't know," I said, with a slightly hysterical rise on the last word.

"You're quite right to go quietly down to the country," Cokie soothed me. "It's not only being bombed with the babies. It's the strain of your husband's illness on top of your own."

"But the girl's working for the Germans," I almost screamed. "It couldn't be anything else. They're measuring up for an airfield in the Isle of Wight for Hitler's invasion forces."

"D'you think you ought to travel alone?" Cokie asked.

"Tell Donald to ring me," I said coldly.

When he did he listened carefully but, to my consternation, took the same line as Cokie, seeming to imply that the bombing had sent me round the bend and made me imagine Marjory Crow.

"I know it's an odd name," I tried to defend myself. "But that's the one she gave, and the rest happened here, on your typewriter. Your Ministry's always warning us with posters against fifth columnists, and now I'm offering you one on a plate, you don't believe there are any."

Donald made soothing noises and returned to the necessity of my leaving London that day.

"Anyway," I gave him my parting shot, "she's going to come and cook your breakfast for you."

But she never turned up. And I never found out for sure whether Donald did or did not do anything about her suspicious activities. All I ever got out of Cokie, when I asked her some time later, was "You poor girl—completely cuckoo!"

* * * * *

The rectory is four miles from the sea. In peacetime the Paris planes fly over the house with comforting regularity. Now the air force flew over the house in greater numbers, almost as regularly. So did the Luftwaffe. It was no use people saying "ours" or "theirs". They all sounded the same to me. The nearest siren cooed softly over the marshes from time to time, but seemed to have no bearing on what went over.

My father wore his tin hat with his black alpaca cassock indoors and out. My mother was very sceptical about the German raiders getting across the Channel at all.

"Once," she said, "one got across and dropped some tiny little bombs on Eastbourne and then landed and gave himself up. He was hardly out of the sixth form."

There was a fifteen-miles-from-the-coast ban on non-residents; and my mother was determined to keep all the secrets behind it.

"Then what's that whacking great crater down in the field over there?" I asked.

"One of ours," she assured me. "They dropped it by mistake on their way out."

"Just as uncomfortable all the same to be hit by it."

"Anyway that was ages ago. They're much more practised now."

As she spoke there was an enormous explosion on the marshes.

"Marsh gas, I suppose?" I teased her.

"Oh, that was only one of their radar huts down there blowing up. They're always so careless. Where are my garden-shears?"

All night long, aeroplanes filled the air with crescendos of throbbing.

"You look really tired," my mother said at breakfast, which we ate in the kitchen with the postman. "Did the baby keep you awake?"

After breakfast I telegraphed Lucy to ring me up. She was at the cottage in which I had stayed with her during the big blitz. Arbuthnot's wife, Nita, was also there; and together they looked after Lucy's baby, Iona, and ran one of the farms on the estate. Lucy got my telegram at lunchtime.

"Lucy, this time I know it's fright," I said. "Can I bring the babies for a bit to get some sleep?"

"Come at once," said Lucy. "We could do with a wife to cook the midday meal and look after Iona, when it's too wet to take her out in the fields."

We passed through London next day. I took the babies to our doctor and learned that they had thread-worm. I had never heard of it before, but presumed it must be caused by my own neglect, carelessness, and lack of efficiency. Pneumonia, bombing, and the fifth column were serious things: but this was the last straw. It seemed such a deep disgrace that I wondered whether I dare disclose this final—and at present greatest—worry to Lucy and Nita. I sat in Paddington Station with the two babies and the kitten and my bicycle and the pram, and felt I had reached the lowest ebb.

All the way to Moreton-in-Marsh this new albatross hung heavily about my neck.

Lucy and Nita met us at the station, with a smart, rich-looking friend and her healthy-looking baby, George, who was being brought up with the care and attention I wished I had known how to give to my own poor contaminated children.

"Oh, Lucy," the smart friend reminded her, "don't forget to stop for George's worm powders."

More beautiful words I could not have hoped to hear.

Lucy had turned out of her room to give us the greatest comfort and for the first time in weeks I slept in undisturbed peace.

We woke to a bright spring day. Lucy and Nita were just going off to the farm. Iona, blonde and sun-tanned, waddled about the little garden mixing earth with water and water with sunflower-seeds. Marian went out to help.

I still felt like a tightly-wound clock—another turn and the spring would snap. But here there would be no turn. Slowly, in this carefree atmosphere, I should unwind. I got up without hurry and lingered pleasantly over Rachel's morning bath.

15

THE BEAUTIFUL moated Elizabethan manor house belonging to Lucy's family had been requisitioned by the army and was now the headquarters of an American tank division. The general paid a formal call at the cottage a few days after we arrived. He looked like a naughty village choirboy; or he might have been a genial pirate: his ears had been pierced for ear-rings.

He and his staff colonel sat balancing cups of tea on their knees, under a line of dripping washing strung across the room where we cooked, ate, sat and entertained.

This was followed by an invitation for all three of us to dine at the Manor. The General, would provide an experienced baby-sitter and send for us in a staff car any night of the week we liked.

"I don't quite see how we can get out of it," Lucy sighed. "And I suppose we ought to go, as it's the Manor."

So we went. After suitable drinks in the General's bed-sitting-room, we were led into the dining-room where twenty-two officers sat at trestle tables beneath portraits of Lucy's family's horses. There we ate great chunks of roast beef, washed down with coffee—poured from a teapot—and rye whisky. During the sweet, "rassberry shortcake" (ordinary army cake with jam on it), all twenty-two officers rose to their feet and sang the birthday song in Nita's honour, to her acute embarrassment.

The General escorted us home himself and asked us to call upon him at any time that we might need the aid of a fine body of men.

The unwinding process progressed. I even began to feel at ease about Donald, who wrote saying he felt better with the spring sunshine. The raids, he said, had not been so bad since we left London.

* * * * *

"Blast!" said Lucy one morning over a letter. "I shall have to go to London tomorrow."

"I can't sow the top field without you," said Nita. "So I might as well come too, while we've got Verily here to look after Iona." I was used to having a third baby; and the day without Lucy and Nita went easily enough.

After tea I bathed the three little girls and put Rachel into her cot. Marian and Iona romped round the fire in their dressing-gowns, their gold curly hair shining after the weekly hairwash. I put them to bed in a happy mood. Marian woke up screaming.

"It's an ow," she told me, "a awful ow."

"Where? In your tummy?"

"No, no. A ow. A awful ow."

"In your head?"

"A ow," she repeated.

I took her temperature and it was high. I crushed half an aspirin and offered it to her in a warm drink. But she could not drink it. Quite suddenly she stopped crying.

"Look! A choo-choo!" she said in a high, unnatural voice. I turned round to see nothing but a chest of drawers. "It's got lights. It's going faster. Look! A elephant!" When she had seen practically a whole circus and discussed it in this staccato voice, panic seized me. All the sights and sounds and smells associated with Donald's sickroom came back to me, as I looked down at that hot, bright-eyed little creature, chattering away in that odd voice.

This seemed to be the moment to avail ourselves of the General's offer, and to go to the Manor and telephone for a doctor. For once I should have to break the rule of never leaving the children alone in a house. But I dared not leave Marian in my bed, free to roam out into the frosty night if the whim took her. Iona was sound asleep: so I lifted her into the baby's cot and laid her beside the baby, and then carried Iona's high-sided cot down to the warmth of the kitchen. I put Marian into it with the diamond pendant. There was nothing else I knew she wanted so much to play with. No toys were buyable at that time, and she had often asked for it. She set busily about trying to take it to pieces.

I went out into the dark and climbed over the wall into the Manor park, risking, so I believed, being shot by a sentry. But the sentry was playing nap with some pals over a bottle of Bourbon, and I was able to walk straight across the bridge and into the house. A young officer told me where to find the telephone and then kindly got the doctor's number for me. The doctor was out.

"Wait here a while and ring him again," suggested the young officer, who introduced himself as Hank. His hair had been cut in the American army style all of a length, giving it the texture of a cat's fur. But he had a kind voice.

"I can't wait," I said, "but I wonder whether you would mind ringing him later."

"I know," said Hank. "We've a doctor of our own. He'll be in soon. I'll bring him over. You're not walking, are you?"

"Yes."

"I'll drive you back. We Americans only use our legs where cars or tanks won't go, inside a house for instance."

I was glad to get back so soon. It was a relief to find Marian still in Iona's cot. She still moved and chatted jerkily.

About an hour later Hank turned up with two other officers. The doctor was of Spanish extraction, dark with lazy brown eyes.

All three started to examine Marian: but she would let none of them get within a foot of her. To her it was a game.

"Does she always roll her eyes like that?" the doctor asked.

I could hardly say "Only when she flirts with soldiers."

The doctor sighed.

"Probably cerebral meningitis," he said, lightly tapping the cot with his cane. "We get packets of it in the States."

In this country I was sure we did not get packets of it. I tried to think if I had ever known of a case. Yes, one, in the village at home. She was now an idiot.

"What is cerebral meningitis?" I asked, hoping it was something different in the States.

"Aw," he said, shaking his head and unable to tell me. It must be the same.

"Can't we get her into hospital?" I asked urgently.

"No point in hospitalising her till we're certain. A sure sign is if the child throws her head back in sleep. Watch out for that. I'll look in again early."

Hank had disappeared into the kitchen. Now he returned with the teapot and cups. Out of it he poured black coffee, into which he shook a generous swig of Cognac.

"You'll need this," he said. I drank it while he poured out the same mixture for the others and himself. I asked them to help me carry Iona's cot upstairs, while I carried Marian.

"I could sit here all night, if you liked," offered Hank.

"Oh, no thank you," I assured him. "I shall be all right."

I was glad of the coffee, for Marian was wakeful and needed my full attention. At last she settled down to sleep, and I lay on my bed without undressing. But I could not sleep in the clutches of this new and terrible fear. Not so long ago I had believed that nothing could frighten me again.

At seven o'clock I got up to look at her once more. She was fast asleep on her side, her bright curls lying softly on the pillow—and her head thrown right back.

I ran down the cottage stairs and out of the door. I scrambled over the wall, wishing I had not been too prudish to accept Hank's offer to stay with us. I ran through the dewy grass and pattered over the bridge into the unguarded house. A sleepy G.I. shuffled down the stairs.

"I want the doctor—quickly!" I said.

While I was waiting for him I telephoned Donald in London. He was not at his club. I telephoned his Ministry and left a message with a porter to tell him to come at once. I felt sick with fear, and my hands trembled so much I could hardly replace the receiver.

Then I telephoned Lucy.

"Have you had the doctor?"

"Yes, one of the Americans."

"Why didn't you get Dr. Houghton? He understands children."

"I tried. I couldn't get him."

"We'll come back," said Susan, "but, V, don't flap."

"Try to bring Donald," I said.

Don't flap, I told myself, don't flap. I shut my eyes and tried to induce calm. Dead or mad! was the only thought I could get into or out of my brain.

The American doctor and his two friends drove me back to the cottage. They woke Marian and she began to scream. The three Americans shook their heads.

"We'll go back and consult the authorities," the doctor said. "Who are the medical authorities around here?" he added.

"I don't know," I said. "I don't even know where the nearest hospital is."

"We'll take care of all that," Hank said. "You just take it easy." He left the remains of the cognac on the table.

I dressed and fed the other two babies in between rushing upstairs to look at Marian. She was awake but quiet. Twice she was sick.

Hank came back to say plans were going ahead. On the way he poured out a cognac and held it up.

"No, thank you," I assured him. He drank it himself.

At midday Lucy's car pulled up outside the cottage. Lucy and Nita came in, followed by Donald.

"Trust V," said Lucy. Iona waddled out to meet them, beaming and well. Lucy looked relieved.

Another car stopped outside. A fair-haired young man with a big scarf ambled up the path like an amiable teddy bear.

"Who's that?" I asked nervily.

"Dr. Houghton. I rang him up from London and asked him to come."

"But the American doctor—" Even at a time like this I remembered that doctors have their etiquette; and the Americans were all three devoting themselves to the case.

"Good morning, everybody," Dr. Houghton said cheerfully. "A little girl is it? Don't bother. I know my way up." He trotted up the stairs. I started to follow.

"Leave him," said Nita. "He's wonderful with children. He gets on better with them alone. He'll probably tell her the three bears."

Lucy and Nita began looking round for letters and things they had left behind, in the way people do who have just been away. Donald said nothing, but appeared distressed to find me in a worse state of consternation than when he last saw me.

"What's all this?" Nita asked, looking out of the window. "A jeep?"

The three Americans were coming up the path. Their helmets clanked as they took them off. They walked straight into the kitchen. I waved my hand across them by way of a general introduction. It was all I could do.

The American doctor slapped his calves with his cane, as he began to explain his plans for bringing one of the American army ambulances round to take Marian to a hospital, which he had at last located. Hank poured out a round of cognac. Dr. Houghton came tripping happily down the stairs, swinging his stethoscope.

"Nasty little go of tonsilitis," he said. "I'll look in to-morrow."

It was as if I had suddenly found I could fly. And yet—

"I'll go up and see her," said Donald quietly.

"Who was that guy?" asked Hank, of Dr. Houghton's retreating back.

"Just a friend," said Lucy, grinning.

"Have another drink," said Hank.

"You'll need to wrap her up warm for the journey," said the American doctor.

"Why not give it another day?" suggested Lucy tactfully.

"Now we're at home, one of us could nip her over in a minute to hospital if she gets any worse," said Nita.

"I *would* prefer to see more of the case myself," the American doctor admitted. "I've never seen one before."

Donald crept down again.

"She's all right," he said to me alone. "We can trust Houghton."

"But her head—right back on her pillow?"

"She always sleeps like that when she's got a cold."

"Finish the bottle," said Hank.

"Thank you," I said gratefully, and sat down.

It *was* a nasty go of tonsilitis, very nasty. Donald sat up with Marian all the next night; and she was ill for a fortnight. I soon had complete confidence in Dr. Houghton; and the Americans came daily and were very pleased to feel that they had all three cured her.

Donald came down for another week-end and made it clear that we must not return to London yet.

"We can't stay here for ever," I said. "Lucy's turned out of her room for us, and we're making her pretty uncomfortable on our behalf."

"We'll find a cottage down here," said Donald.

"Darling," I said bitterly, "we've got a whacking great house in St. John's Wood and a room at the club. We can't have a cottage in the country as well. What about our overdraft? And have you seen the bills?"

"Yes, love. I have seen the bills. That's why I've stopped living at the club."

"You sleep at home?"

"I sleep on the floor of my office."

"Oh, darling!" I exclaimed, shocked. "After pneumonia!"

"It's quite warm."

"But how do you eat?"

"In the Ministry canteen."

"Surely it would be better if we all went back home?"

"No, darling. You know it wouldn't. We should never have kept Marian in the air-raids long enough to be frightened. The house will have to go."

"Oh, no," I said unhappily. "Not another home when we've just settled in."

"I'm afraid so, sweetheart. But I know you'll make a lovely new one here. You've made some pretty good ones already."

"But you won't be in it."

"I shall. For week-ends and my summer leave."

In only a few days Nita had found a partly-furnished farm-house two miles from the village. The farm was in the hands of a bailiff; and once again we were offered a house at a low rent to prevent requisitioning. Nita took me to see it in the dog-cart.

We drove along more than a mile of cart-track to reach it. But once there you could not conceive a more lovely position. Views of the distant hills and of fields and woods below reassured me that I had not lost my capacity to be deeply moved by beauty as well as by fear. In the heart of the Cotswold country this old grey stone house stood between the farmyard and a low-walled garden. Meadows and orchards sloped down to a shallow stream.

That evening I telephoned Donald about the farmhouse.

"It would be perfect," I said, "if it weren't so big."

"Take it," he said. "A friend knows a young widow, with a baby of Ton-Ton's age, who wants to share expenses in the country."

Lucy and Nita agreed to look after Marian and Rachel while I went to London for one night to pack up our house. We had spent just about the same amount of time on making this home as we had on our first flat; and now it had to be dismantled with very little time to do it in.

It was so wonderful to be home again, cooking Donald's supper in my own kitchen and sitting by our own fireside, that I wasted several good working hours arranging flowers I had brought from the country and just living as though we were going to stay there for ever, as we had hoped to do.

"But the farmhouse sounds lovely, darling," Donald tried to comfort me.

Early next morning I began to pack.

I was grateful for such havoc as the bombs and incendiaries had caused. At least it gave me somewhere to start. Broken glass had to be picked out of carpets and bedding. Some of our things were not worth salvaging. Donald helped till it was time to go to the office; and then Cokie came along to lend a hand. Cokie was a great asset, both physically and psychologically. She trundled well-filled trunks and suitcases down the stairs without stopping her conversation to get breath. She had none of my illusions over the sanctity of this particular home.

"Come along, dear, strip them down," she said of the curtains. I had finished making them only a few days before our flight. "Never mind about the pelmets, ducks. Rip them off. They'll do for dusters." Ten-and-six a yard and all hemmed by hand, I thought, but I did as she said.

She soon persuaded me to leave our six-foot-by-six double bed behind, to go into an auction she knew about.

"No wonder my poor boss turns up at the office with rings under his eyes," said Cokie. "It's all the wrong shape for comfort. It's more like a raft."

"We'll have nothing to sleep on but a couple of black iron bedsteads that my mother took from her old home for her maids when she was married."

"No maids would ever sleep on those nowadays," she said, looking them over. "You might just as well use them yourselves and get a little individual sleep at last."

"And the big pram," said Cokie. "Put that in the auction too. It won't be any use in cart-ruts. You've still got the little one."

When Cokie had established in me an urge for destruction in place of my mood of nostalgic admiration, she left me to get on with it, promising to return before I left.

At first I was systematic about packing, but gradually, as the time of my train drew nearer, I became desperate and threw tennis-shoes and Oxo cubes and sal volatile all in together. Cokie came back to find me trying to force all the family's coat-hangers into an already over-filled suitcase.

"It's no good," I said. "I shall have to leave them. Would they be any use to you?"

"Twenty-two coat-hangers? No thank you, dear. My own flat went up on Wednesday with part of Paddington Station, and I haven't anywhere to put anything. As it was, they had to fetch me down with a ladder."

"It's a pity to waste them," I said. "Could you take them to a cousin who lives near here? There are some of her sheets she lent us when Donald was ill, to go too. Oh, and I can't hope to pack the pot of bulbs in the bathroom."

"Of course, dear."

I gave her my cousin's address.

Cokie said afterwards that never, in the whole war, was her morale so reduced as when she walked up the steps of my cousin's highly respectable preparatory school, with her taxi ticking up behind her, bearing the pot of bulbs. I had not explained that the bulbs were electric ones and the pot of the common bedroom type.

Donald turned up just as I was about to leave. I could hear his footsteps moving about the house as he had a last look round. Together we slammed the front door and went down the steps hand in hand.

16

AT FIRST our London furniture looked ill at ease in the old stone farmhouse, particularly the bombed and reconditioned Victorian. But in a few days it was mingling happily with milking-stools, mole-traps, nose-bags, and the other essential country accessories that lay about the house. Choopy was adaptable too and soon learned the joys of hunting, bringing home rabbits nearly as big as himself and laying them at my feet for the pot.

The wife of the cowman, who worked on the farm, came to examine us from time to time. Having "done" for the owner of the farm, she allowed herself free access to the house. She was thin and her skin had a queer browny-grey colour. She would lean on a long-handled shovel, which she always produced from somewhere to give the kitchen drain a good poke out, when she came to inspect us.

"Not a very healthy place for children," she observed on her maiden visit.

"Oh, but it's lovely!" I contradicted her. "Perfect for them."

"Too much open air don't suit them," she went on mournfully. "If you'd seen the little coffins I had . . ."

Marian, as soon as she recovered from the nasty little go of tonsilitis, which left her looking pale and trampled on and given to frightful nightmares, settled in as though she had always lived there, and responded to the open air in the way I hoped for. She was born for the country. Rachel, now a year old and like a china doll, was prepared to be cheerful and friendly anywhere.

But, alas, the young widow supplied by Donald could clearly never adapt herself. She came down to breakfast on her first cold spring morning, which we had planned to devote to unpacking, dressed as for a cocktail party, with chic little high-heeled snake-skin shoes. Jewellery clanked about her person and her make-up scented the ancient kitchen, used to nothing stronger than frying onions and mouldering hams. She was taller than I, but by nature a little woman, to be protected as much from herself as from anybody. I liked her at once and we got on well together, but my mother, who was staying with us to help move in, was much puzzled by her. She called my mother Mummy, because, she said sadly, she could never remember having one of her own. My mother had never been called Mummy before, and it fussed her.

The young widow's dainty little girl, Alison, was the most advanced child of eighteen months I have ever seen. She sang long and complicated songs, was house-trained, tap-danced, and deliberately kept her frocks clean. The only thing she could not do was eat. Rachel still knocked back several bottles a day, swallowed anything that was put into her mouth on a spoon, and with her fingers stuffed in such food as she found lying about, often settling down beside the cat's food in a business-like way. But if I offered Alison food she only turned her head away and retched delicately.

At every meal her mother stood over her and would first try to tempt her, then jolly her, then plead, then storm, then weep, and finally throw the food at her. Alison sat looking up at her with round wide beautiful eyes and a wistful expression, but eat she would not.

Both had been fairly badly blitzed (they were still marred by stitches) and no doubt this affected Alison's appetite. The regular scenes her mother made finished off any desire in Alison to see, smell, or hear about food.

"Children always eat for me," my mother claimed. "Let me try her."

"All right, Mummy," the smart young widow said tearfully. "Take the spoon."

"But you must go away," my mother stipulated.

"You promise you won't force her?" The widow went.

My mother put a fresh bowl of vegetables and gravy in front of Alison, and walked away to the other end of the kitchen and began washing up.

"You dry," she told me. "And don't appear to take any notice."

From where I stood I could see Alison pick up a spoon, stir the food round a bit, look at it, poke it, and then pick up a piece of carrot in her fingers. Whereupon her mother, who had been watching through a crack in the door, rushed in.

"Alison! Put that down this instant! What do you think your spoon's for? What disgusting manners!" Alison naturally obeyed, and did not pick up any more.

By the time my mother left, the smart young widow had ceased to find the farmhouse quaint. It was two miles' walk to the village shop. We were not on the telephone. We had no electricity, and had to pump the water ourselves. We cooked on a range in a kitchen as high—and often as cold—as a church. Fulsome smells floated up from the cowsheds to our bedroom windows. The cows themselves were known to wander in.

The widow yearned for London, bombs and all. She started to talk about going back.

Apart from Alison's need to be out of the blitz, I wanted them to stay for my own sake. The widow was no earthly use in a house, but she had agreed to share expenses: moreover, just that very morning I had learned from the lugubrious wife of the cowman that the ghost of a seven-foot shepherd was said to haunt the long hall passage.

"I must go," the widow cried in her longing. "I must! I promise I'll come back. I must, just for one night."

"Then need you take Alison?"

"Would you have her?" she asked in grateful surprise. "If you would, maybe we could make it two nights."

"No," I said firmly. "I can only endure one night of terror."

"Terror? But there aren't any bombs here."

"I mean anxiety—" I corrected myself quickly, not wanting to add to the farmhouse's list of inconveniences, "—for you while you're in London."

"Then I'll go on Thursday. Whoopee!" She rushed off to wash her hair.

I prepared for Thursday, getting in aspirin and more paraffin, so that I could leave a light on all night. I moved all three cots into my room, as though against an air-raid. Choopy also must sleep with us.

On Wednesday the baker brought a telegram with the bread.

It was from Julie. She was arriving today with James and her new baby. In fact they must already be at the station.

"Hold on!" I shouted to the baker. "We want a lift."

"Whoah up!" he instructed his horse, while I gathered up Marian and Rachel, wiped their faces, and lifted them into the van. I climbed up after them.

"We're going to the village to try and get the taxi," I called to the widow. "A girl friend's coming to stay."

How good the freshly baked bread smelt! How gaily the birds sang now that I should not have to battle with the seven-foot shepherd alone!

"Look at all the little monkeys," cried Marian happily, pointing to a field of new-born lambs frisking round their mothers. Her education in animals had been gained at the London Zoo.

In the village we were able to transfer to the taxi. At Moreton-in-Marsh station we found Julie sitting peacefully on her suitcase with the baby on her knee and James, curly-headed and adorable, standing beside her.

"It was a landmine," she explained. "I hope you don't mind our coming. I couldn't think what else to do."

"Mind? It's marvellous. I don't know what I'd have done if you hadn't come." I told her about the smart young widow. "You will stay a bit, won't you?" I looked at her one modest suitcase.

"Stay?" she repeated. "I should think I will. I'm here for the duration."

"So am I."

The widow was not the least bit put off by Julie's description of the night before in London. She took the taxi back to the station.

"It seems such a waste not to," she called out of the window. "And I expect one night or two will be all the same to you."

She was away about a week.

When we bathed Alison, Julie and I were distressed to find how emaciated she was; although, if left alone, she picked a little at small amounts of food. Next time Dr. Houghton called I showed her to him.

"Keep the mother away at all costs," he said, "if you want this child to live." He told me he had come across other cases like this in which the mother had passed on her own war-nerves to her child. "A child as weak as this is open to all sorts of infections."

The cowman's lugubrious wife, scenting out trouble like a terrier after rats round a bran-bin, came and tut-tutted over Alison.

"If they're not good doers, nothing won't make them do," she said. "That poor Mrs. Marrow down by the stream always buried hers in white."

The widow left no address: so we feared every day she would return and undo the little good we could do. Then, as the doctor predicted might happen, Alison contracted some strange infection of the bowel and became so ill that we did all we could to get her mother back. When she turned up, spry and gay and still with an aura of the West End of London about her, she was so alarmed by her baby's illness that we wished she had not come.

"It's all her own fault!" she cried. "She wouldn't eat, and I told her she'd be ill." She dashed in to Alison's cot; and I expected her to shake her. But now she hugged her and kissed her, until Alison fell back on her pillow exhausted.

The widow said she could not bear illness. She would get a friend to come and nurse her baby. She herself had better go back to London where she would be more in touch with good specialists. We agreed.

The friend turned up, a square, forthright north-country-woman, who knew how kitchens should be kept and how sick babies should be nursed. Starvation, that was what a sick child, or a sick puppy for that matter, needed to put it to rights. Then a good strong dose of salts. Julie and I, who were determined to keep Alison alive, had to keep sneaking in with fruit, which Dr. Houghton had told us to give her. When it came to the good strong dose of salts, luckily Alison herself resumed her hunger strike.

Although the friend advocated starvation for sick babies and puppies, she had other plans for her own eleven-year-old son, whom she brought with her. Never was a child more wilfully stuffed than he was. All our week's rations went into him during their first twenty-four hours with us. Our carefully saved babies' egg ration was set before him at breakfast, all three of them; and, as he started to eat the first boiled egg, his mother leaned across the table and popped the last of our butter ration into it.

"That's what I like about the country," she said. "You can nourish a child."

Julie and I could not bring ourselves to break it to her that you could *not*, with a war on—even in a farmhouse. She soon found out.

At last Alison recovered sufficiently for them all to go away; but within a week of returning to her mother and the bombs she was ill again, I heard, and had to spend a long period in hospital, where she forgot her songs and her tap-dancing but put on enough weight to survive.

Marian and James settled down in their old twin routine. They trotted about the garden and farmyard together, leading each other into fairly harmless mischief.

"Come and look out of the window," Julie called me into her bedroom one morning. Down in the farmyard, climbing up a heap of manure, were Marian and James one behind the other. Marian was swamped by a huge felt hat with a chimney-like crown. James wore a small black straw hat with an eye veil. I had paid pounds for those, my only two, hats. To Julie's everlasting delight I was furious.

"How dare they!" I stormed, and rushed down to recover my hats and deliver a scolding.

"You old spoil-sport!" Julie called out of the window. Marian and James were now coming down the other side of the manure heap, looking as innocent as daisies. But I got my hats and they got their scolding.

One Sunday morning, when both our husbands were at the farmhouse for the week-end, Malcolm complained that the tea tasted of paraffin. "Nonsense," we said, "we've just drunk some: it was all right." Donald said the porridge tasted of paraffin. "Ours didn't," we said. Both refused their kippers on the grounds of paraffin. "The kippers were delicious," we insisted.

It was some time before we discovered that Marian or James or both had been "cooking" in the kettle, mixing in everything at hand, including paraffin; thus, as we added hot water from the kettle to the tea, porridge, and kippers for the late-risers, they were treated to the added flavour.

With never a searchlight in the sky, never a distant rumble, Julie and I soon became riotously cured of our winter in London. Our only visible or audible enemies now were cats and mice.

The cats came in from the farmyard in herds of what seemed to be hundreds. They were all black and thin and looked the same. The moment our backs were turned they would sidle into the kitchen and make for any food, even if it was still hot in a saucepan. As soon as Julie saw them coming, she would charge down the haunted passage hissing and roaring at them. Choopy, if he was in the line of charge, just stepped politely to one side, knowing that the assault was not for him.

One particularly persistent cat caught us out in the night by coming in and having five kittens in the coal-bucket. In the morning we carried them out to a distant shed. By lunch time the cat had leapt over a six-foot wall with them one by one, bundled them along a roof-top, and brought them all back to the coal-bucket. Every day we would have this battle of the kittens. We carried them to the shed. The cat brought them back. Then we found we had a traitor in the camp. There were four kittens in the coal bucket. The cat was on her way back over the roof for the fifth. Walking across the farmyard, very pleased with herself, was Marian carrying the fifth.

"This one's too little to go that way," she shouted, pointing to the roof.

The mice were quite different. At least the cats knew they were not wanted; but the mice seemed to think we liked them. By night they ran affectionately over our faces as we lay in bed, and by day they settled down in little clusters round the food we had laid out for ourselves. They had no respect for Choopy, who anyway was ham-handed with anything smaller than a young rabbit. Once I opened the kitchen cupboard and reached up for a bag of flour, and a mouse jumped into the opening of my frock and wriggled down inside, emerging to jump on to my feet, which were bare. I was amazed.

Our only other visitors, besides Lucy and Nita and Iona, were the American soldiers. They called in jeeps or armoured cars or even sometimes tanks; and they always brought chocolate for the children and bourbon for us. We let them drink the bourbon, and ate the chocolate ourselves. They loved hearing about the London blitz, so that they could write home and horrify their wives and mothers. And we loved exaggerating our bomb stories for them.

They all seemed genuinely fond of children and often helped us to bath the babies. One night the General came and watched his staff colonel bathing our smallest.

"To think," the General said, wiping a tear from his eye, "that these liddle kids have been under so much gunfire, and I haven't yet been near a baddle . . ." I wondered what all his medals were for.

They all longed to go into battle, and practised doing it in their tanks all over the hayfields and sprouting corn, ruining the crops for miles round. They knew the farmers would be compensated, so they could never quite understand why their manoeuvres caused so much local unpopularity. They were like little boys with dinky toys, loving to crash them about, no matter how much they broke up the nursery. But they were generous with their toys, and took pleasure in lending their tanks to us girls to play with. Thus the staff colonel, after letting one of us take him for a drive in one of his own fighting vehicles, had a leg in plaster of Paris for months; and Julie's sister, Helen, who admitted she had never driven anything but a tractor in a farmyard, when she came to stay crashed an armoured car into a stream.

I was hurried secretly, for fear that Julie would be alarmed, to the hospital tent at the American headquarters, where Helen lay on an operating-table with the Spanish doctor putting stitches into her face.

She greeted me with surprising cheerfulness as I sat down beside her.

"Drink this," said Hank, lifting her head enough to pour another whisky down her throat. Helen had never tasted neat alcohol before. It seemed to have a suitably numbing effect.

"You'll need one too," said Hank, pouring out a lavish drink for me and one for himself.

"So'll I when I'm through," the doctor said, looking round to make sure his needs would be covered.

* * * * *

One wet afternoon I set off across the fields to the village to buy our rations of dried eggs and spam. It had been raining all day and all the night before. On my way home through the woods, I might as well have walked along the middle of the stream, so soaked was I when I got home. I took off my mackintosh and skirt outside the back door, and shook them before I pushed open the door and went in.

Sitting on the kitchen table drinking cups of tea were a number of very young English soldiers. I backed out into the rain again, wondering whether I had come to the wrong house. Julie flew out with a pram rug to wrap round me. Behind her was a good-looking young man wearing the pips of a captain.

"I'm terribly sorry," he said.

"I told them I didn't know whether you'd want them," said Julie.

"The fact is," said the captain, "we got washed out of our tents last night. We've been trying to get dry all day, but it's obviously hopeless, so I've been given orders to billet the cadets—we're Royal Armoured Corps. I've placed two hundred men. These twelve and my batman and me are left over."

"But we haven't got fourteen beds," I said.

"We don't need beds, only a roof. And d'you think we might use your range to cook a meal on?"

"Of course. You all look very wet too," I said. "Have we any male clothes?" I asked Julie.

"There's a trunk of Donald's in the attic," she remembered. I took the captain up with his batman, while Julie organised the cadets into piling fuel on the boiler fire for hot baths.

From the attic we brought down and distributed one tail coat, one dinner jacket, one pair of tennis shoes with holes in the toes, two pairs of riding breeches with moth in them, five pairs of mixed trousers, some jerseys, pyjamas, hunting-boots, and a full-dress tunic.

In these, the freshly bathed gentlemen-cadets sat down with Julie, Marian, James, and myself to a delicious high tea of bacon and four fried eggs apiece.

"We got them cracked from a packing station," the captain explained.

"Tell us where," Julie and I said in one voice.

While Julie and I put the children to bed, five mattresses were hurled down the stairs to make, later on, one vast bed. But it was much too early to turn in yet.

We lit the paraffin lamps early and drew the curtains on the teeming skies outside. Somebody kindled a fire in the parlour. The versatile batman, having washed up in the kitchen, now brought in the third brew of tea and then sat down at the piano and played dance music.

It must have been at about this point that the cowman's sinister wife passed through the farmyard and saw the parked truck and motor bicycles outside our door. Strains, too, of the music must have floated across the cow byres to her suspicious ears.

For a while we danced and talked; and then Julie and I left the cadets to arrange their mattresses and bedding.

"Exercises begin at o-six-double-o," said the captain. "Good night."

The cowman's wife must have been up early to have seen the fourteen soldiers creep out of the house, trying not to wake the babies. I was up to see them off. Last of all went the captain, who, to the delight no doubt of the cowman's wife, gave me money.

She can have wasted no time in hurrying off to the village with the news.

The captain said on parting, "I forgot to tell you last night, you get a billeting allowance for this. Three shillings a head."

Donald came down next day with some young friends. We were all sitting round the fire after supper, when a knock at the garden door made Julie and me think the seven-foot shepherd had come at last.

Julie went to the door. The staff colonel was propping himself on his crutch, with Hank and two others beside him. He held out an expensive bunch of carnations.

"To the darlings of the tank corps of two countries," he said with a stiff bow.

"Really!" said Julie.

"You never asked us to your dance," the staff colonel added in a hurt voice.

"Look here," I came out and started to give the true version of the previous evening's happenings; but they still stood in a row looking like little boys with a grudge because somebody's big brother had borrowed their roller-skates. "Anyway, come in."

They came in with a bit of a bluster, which they dropped when they saw that we were not alone.

"We thought you might like a drink," said Hank, bringing a bottle out of his pocket and some glasses out of the staff colonel's.

"You mean you thought you'd like a little party," said Julie.

"No," said the staff colonel, "we've chosen this house for a meeting tonight of the society of applied practical and theoretical debauchery. Or don't the English drink?"

"The English can't drink," said Donald. "They can't get hold of the stuff."

"Well what do they do with their long winter evenings all the year round?"

"Play games," said Hank, who was an authority on English life in the best circles, coming, as he did, from one of the oldest families of Boston, New England. "Charades and Think Of A Number and Treasure Hunt. Let's play Treasure Hunt."

The other Americans tried to twist their faces into bright looks of willingness, as seen on the faces of children visiting elderly grandparents.

"Yes, let's play Treasure Hunt," they said in flat unison.

"Well," said Hank, "you need vehicles. One for every two players. But that's all right—we've got three outside, and we can pick up some more on the way."

"Can't we play it theoretically round the fire?" suggested Donald, who had a glass of his guest's bourbon in his hand.

"Oh, no! It's all part of the fun, tearing round the countryside at night."

"I'm not tearing round any countryside at night," said Julie firmly. "Somebody's got to sit in here with the children."

"You do that, and I'll help you," the staff colonel volunteered.

"Not likely!" said Julie, even more firmly.

"Then we'll go out in small groups in turn," Hank organised. "Each hunting party has to bring back, let's say, something purple," he ticked off the items on his fingers, "something nobody can think what to do with, and some token of sentimentality."

During the next couple of hours, jeeps and armoured cars milled about the farmyard, bringing back purple hearts and pieces cut off sheep or hammered off motorcars.

Soon only Donald and I and the staff colonel and one shy young American, called Wick, had not yet contributed their treasures. Wick was anxious to start.

We helped the staff colonel into a jeep, and set off to bump over fields and cruise along dark lanes. The English may have had their cars pushed off the roads by petrol rationing: but the Americans had plenty of "gas" left over from their manoeuvring.

"Hi, stop!" the staff colonel cried suddenly.

"Seen a treasure?" Wick asked with some excitement.

"Yes, the Three Doves."

We got out and went into the small village pub and drank some beer. It was nearly closing time.

"Aw, hell," said Wick as we got back into the jeep, "the steering's gone. We'll have to change this jeep. It's the General's own and he'll sure grouch. He hates it being touched."

"Can't he stop it being touched?" Donald asked innocently.

"With all those cars about? And all those boys wanting runs in cars?"

"In the American army," I explained to Donald, "the custom is that if anyone wants a car he just goes to the car park and helps himself. It's known as the call of the wild, or the call of nature, or something."

"Really?" said Donald.

With only the slightest suggestion of steering left, we wound our way back to the American headquarters.

"You wait here," said Wick, putting Donald and me out on to the bridge. "We'll be back."

"Come inside," I said to Donald. "It's cold."

Tonight the sentry was not even playing nap. He had gone away altogether.

"Let's collect a treasure and go home," said Donald. "It's getting late."

"What, though?"

"Anything. Let's get back to that bourbon."

"I know!" I said suddenly, with more enthusiasm for the game, "The General's pyjamas! Hank said the other day they're purple, and if he only grumbles about his jeep being taken he won't mind about his pyjamas. I know where his room is. We sat there when we came to dinner."

We went upstairs. A lot of lights were on, but the house seemed empty. I told Donald how I had stayed there before the war, and pointed out the room I slept in.

The General's light was on. I pushed the door open and beckoned to Donald.

Sitting on his bed, strumming dreamily at his ukulele on his knee, was the General—wearing his purple pyjamas.

"The treasure complete," I said, "purple, can't think what to do with it, and the whole a token of sentimentality."

"Hallo, there," said the General, focusing us with an effort, and making an unsuccessful attempt to rise to his feet. "Come right in and have a drink."

"We've got a small party—" I began.

"Pardy? Pardy?" The general's eyes shone brighter. "Where's the pardy? Where's my stav car?" He rose triumphantly to his bare feet and thumped on the floor with his ukulele.

An orderly came in at the run.

"Bring my stav car to the bridgehead," the general ordered.

"Hey, you'll need a coat if you're going out," said the orderly.

"No, no coat," said the general. "Going to a pardy." He picked up his cane and forage cap and started for the door. Donald picked up his coat and put it on him, and took one arm. I took the other. As we led him down the stairs, singing a little, Wick came into the hall and was appalled by what he saw.

"The General's coming to the party," I said. "He's going to be our treasure."

"I'll be your treasure," the general told me, "Honey!"

"But he can't," Wick objected. "No really. Wouldn't you rather have a party here?" he tried to tempt the General.

"No. Going in my stav car. Where is it?"

"Out here, sir," said his orderly.

The staff colonel was leaning against the front door.

"Oh, good," he approved. "Now the meeting can open."

By the time we had got the General into his car he was asleep. But we lifted him out at the farmhouse and supported him along the haunted passage. We offered him to the company as our contribution.

Our trophy seemed to us to be something you could really call a treasure, a semi-conscious general in purple pyjamas.

But some of our young English visitors, and even Hank, with his New England background, felt it was not quite in good taste.

"After all," somebody said, "he's standing by on duty—almost on parade—so it's not very dignified for him to be taken advantage of like this."

"I've been on parade in pyjamas," said Donald, to ease the embarrassment. Then he spoiled his tactfulness by adding, "—in Poona, in the hot weather." For everyone present knew Poona to be as fictitious as Shangri-La.

* * * * *

All talk now was of the Second Front. Military exercises, not only by the Americans, made the lanes unsafe to walk in. Tanks came roaring along, knocking pieces off houses as they turned corners by skidding. Marian and James, once trapped in their push-chair between a wall that had just been knocked down and an onrush of tanks, asked to be taken to the same place next day "to do it again." But from then on we kept them in the garden.

One early morning I was woken by the creaking of the heavy old door at the end of the passage. I sat up and listened. Muffled and padding steps came up the stairs. Lucy, wearing jodhpurs and her scarlet suede coat, came into the room with her labrador.

"I've brought Iona," she said. "Can you keep her till tomorrow?"

"What's happened?"

"I can't tell you."

I had planned to go to London that day to see Donald, but I pushed the idea aside. I could tell from Lucy's manner that this was even more important.

"Are you going away?" I asked.

"Yes, and Nita. She had an accident yesterday with the tractor and can't do a thing with her hand. So she might as well come." She dumped Iona's night clothes down on a chair. "V, you're not to tell a soul, but a message came through last night."

"From Michael?"

"It didn't say. It just told me where to go. We've got Harden outside in the trap."

I crawled from my bed and looked out of the window. I could see Nita sitting up in the dog-cart with Harden in the shafts. Lucy explained that a rolled-up tent, bedding, food, and a bag of corn were stacked in the back. "Where's Iona now?" I asked.

"She was so sleepy, she hardly noticed we'd brought her. I put her in your pram downstairs and she went straight to sleep again."

I went to sleep again too.

At tea-time next day Lucy turned up on her bicycle. She flopped down on the grass beside me where I was shelling peas.

"You look as though you've seen angels," I said.

"I have," said Lucy, and buried her face in the grass and chuckled.

"Can you tell me?"

"I think so, now it's over, though I suppose it still comes roughly under the heading of careless talk."

"What happened?"

"Well, you saw us go. It was such a lovely beautiful day, V, and I knew I was going to see Michael. We went through country I never knew existed: all the fruit blossom out, and we could hear the cuckoo against Harden's clop-clop on the lanes. We crossed glinting streams and followed cart-tracks between reddy brown ploughs, with the corn sprouting. I got out and walked up the hills, and Nita got out to open the gates. We stopped once or twice to rest Harden, and lay on our backs in the warm sun. It was so soothing to anyone as excited as I was. We reached the village the message told us to go to, and the pub couldn't put us up. It didn't matter, we had the tent.

"We made a camp near a wood, and a girl came over to us looking as though she was going to complain. But by a bit of luck I recognised her. We'd been at school together. After that nothing was too good for us. She moved us on to their lawn and we had supper with them. Her father ran the Home Guard and they all knew what was going to happen early next day, though at first they didn't know that's why we'd come, and were very secretive.

"It was her father who woke us next morning. We could hear him shrieking, 'The sky's full of them!' It was. Khaki and all sorts of bright-coloured parachutes everywhere. This was the first lot. We were told there would be more. We pressed up to the top of the hill a mile and a half away. I was shaking so much I could hardly climb over a big wall, and Nita was one-handed, so some-how I had to heave her over too.

"The aeroplanes came over in threes, and suddenly, out of the last lot, we saw a parachute in the air again. We were wildly excited. Then hundreds of them all coming down with equipment on different-coloured parachutes. You could see the men actually jumping, V. Then they got caught in the slipstream or something, and were tugged back a bit and twisted about roughly. Then they dropped like stones till the parachutes unfurled, righted them-selves, and floated exquisitely down to earth. The beauty of it, apart from everything else, was unbelievable.

"One failed to open properly and came down four times as fast as the others. I clutched Nita and said, 'It must be Michael!' But of course it wasn't.

"We watched them all jump, landing in the next field with their chutes flying out behind them, unbuckling their parachute coats, then searching for their equipment by looking for the right colour. One man asked us, 'Seen a bit of blue silk?'

"Then suddenly some more were coming down right on top of us. We ran to the wall for cover. Several dropped very near and one within twenty yards. We turned to see another drop behind us, and heard 'Oi!' It was Michael, staggering, running towards us unbuttoning his parachute coat as he ran. He cast it off with his parachute. He was grinning like he does. I just stood rooted to the spot. I couldn't move or speak. Michael kissed me and then Nita, but we couldn't find a place free of harness to kiss him properly back. His batman landed near, young and fluffy and giggling over the kissing. Michael rallied his men and charged off into action over the wall, leaving us spellbound.

"We tried on his parachute coat and harness and decided we looked like old-fashioned bathing girls. Then we trapped back in a trance. That's all, V, and here we are."

* * * * *

On June 6th Marian and James came rushing in from the garden.

"Aeroplanes! Two tied together!" James cried.

"Huge," said Marian, glad of a chance to use her new word.

The sky was vibrating with sound. We ran out on to the lawn. None of us had seen aeroplanes since we came to the Cotswolds. Now they moved in a continuous stream over us.

"They're towing gliders," said Julie. "James is right."

"It's our invasion!" I said, jumping up and down. "It can't be anything else. We've invaded France!"

We ran across the meadow to the cowman's wife. She had the nearest radio. We had never asked to listen to it before.

"Yes, it's the invasion all right," she said. "They've landed in Portugal. Hundreds of our poor boys killed."

"Portugal?" I repeated.

"Some such name."

One of the many thrilling broadcasts about the Normandy landings was in progress.

"Could it be Normandy?" I suggested.

"Yes, Normandy. Same thing no doubt. They're all foreign places."

The broadcast was stirring and real and near. Not many hours after the first landings, we were hearing intimate details and recordings. It put us, with all the millions of listeners throughout the world, right in it. I wondered whether our paratroopers landing on strange French fields, not knowing what hedge hid the enemy, felt the influence and blessing of those millions.

We walked slowly back over the meadow. This was the day for which we had waited for four years. And now I, for one, felt drained of feeling.

17

NOW THAT the invasion had begun and more and more troops were being poured into France, our Americans became nearly frantic with frustration. They were sure they had been forgotten, and feared that they might be left behind altogether.

For the first few days after D Day, they never left the Manor in case their orders came to embark. But gradually they strayed further and further afield, and fell back into their old habits of helping themselves to vehicles from the collection, which had been sorted into the right order for departure, all facing the same way. The normal jumble returned. The G.I.s went back to the village pub, and life was resumed at the Manor as before.

Stirred up by D Day, Julie and I felt we should be doing more for our country than merely raising our own young. We offered to help on the farm. Our first job was to weed a field of turnips with a horse-hoe. We left the pram by a hedge, with Marian and James playing round it, and got to work.

"The trouble is," I said to Julie as we bumped over the brow of the hill, "I can't tell which are the weeds and which are the turnips."

"Don't let that worry you," said Julie, struggling to release a tangled rein from under the horse's hoof. "I can't tell which is the horse and which is the harness. They both seem to be made of the same materials."

Donald came down for a few days' leave. He was followed by Alan, one of his Minister's two young secretaries, who had become friends of ours.

Alan was brought to the house by one of the Americans, who fetched him for us from the station. He was looking pale and worried.

"You look as though you've seen a ghost, Alan," I said.

"What I've seen is as good as a ghost," said Alan, settling down in a deck-chair on the lawn with a glass of local cider. "It'll be in the papers tomorrow, so there's no harm in telling you."

He described the terrifying robot-controlled aeroplane filled with high-explosive that German scientists had devised. The Ministry were busy trying to think of a less alarming name for it than those invented by the London press—"Manless Machine", "Pilotless Aircraft", "Hitler's Victory Weapon".

"Really, Alan," I said, "you must all be very short of work to worry about names for Men from Mars. Such a thing couldn't possibly work, however much Hitler wanted it to."

"Couldn't it?" said Alan. "Then how d'you account for several of the brutes reaching London, cutting out their engines, diving, and bursting with as much force as a block-buster?"

He went on describing the new terror, until the rest of us looked and felt as worried as he.

"Even if it doesn't burst dangerously near you," said Alan, "it's jolly unnerving to hear the thing chugging overhead and then suddenly go eerily silent—and you know that in five seconds there'll be an almighty explosion. It's much worse than ordinary bombs. I'm afraid these things are going to do a vast amount of damage. There's no stopping them."

"Someone will work out an antidote," said Donald. "They always do. The all-conquering weapon will never be invented."

"I hope you're right—about this one," said Alan. "I want to relax. It's jolly peaceful here."

After a good night's rest, Alan was more cheerful about the situation and we all had a pleasant week-end. Yet, when I saw him and Donald off across the fields early on Monday morning to catch the village bus, I felt pangs of fear returning as they headed for the reception end of this new warfare. But Donald was excited. He wanted to see for himself what the new weapon was like and what it did and how counter-action would be taken.

From then on, friends and relations from London and the south of England frequently came down to us for a few days' rest from the exhausting strain of the flying bombs.

Julie and I handed over the horse-hoe to our visitors, as a counter-irritant for their frayed nerves, and decided that for the present our war-work had better lie in feeding them so that they could work well on the farm.

Our ever-helpful Americans fetched them from the station and returned them and gave parties for them with fork suppers—and Hank was always at hand with a bottle.

* * * * *

Good news of the successful fighting in France was soon cancelled out for me by much less agreeable news that came in a letter from our bank manager, forwarded by Donald. Our over-draft was now, the letter ran, quite out of proportion. Would we please state what steps we proposed to take for immediate repayment of the whole amount? And then, would we kindly refrain from drawing cheques unless the account held an adequate credit balance to meet them?

Such a letter received in London would have had the effect of sending me straight out to buy something unnecessary, just to give me confidence. But, marooned as I was in the Cotswold hills, surrounded by cows in fields instead of obliging shop-assistants in shops, its impact seemed to hit me right below the belt.

It's not fair, I thought, disregarding the money the bank had trusted us with, against very scanty security. How could we possibly repay such a sum all at once? It amounted to a quar-ter of Donald's annual income. And what were we to live on, if I could not sign cheques?

Donald's covering letter did nothing to allay my sense of injustice and disaster. "It was bound to come sooner or later," he wrote, with infuriating dispassion. "There were all our moves, and hospital and doctors' bills for the pair of us. But chiefly we can blame our own carelessness and optimism." I was in no mood to blame myself for anything.

Worse still, Donald calmly wrote, "We must think what to do about it."

Thinking about it was not nearly good enough for me. Seen through my impulsively anxious eyes, action, not thought, was the only way to save us.

"We can discuss it next time I come down," Donald's letter went on.

But that would not be for three weeks. Meanwhile my babies would die of starvation! I began to panic.

I half-walked and half-ran the two miles to the telephone kiosk in the village, and spent what I believed to be our last few shillings on something that seemed to me to be the prime necessity of the moment, a call to Donald.

"Hold hard, darling," he interrupted my rating of his callousness towards his children and wife. "There are two things we can do. One is, to borrow. But that means repaying sometime, and it wouldn't really get us out of our difficulty. The other thing is to go on paying my salary into the bank, and not draw anything out till the overdraft is paid off."

"But the manager wants it all immediately."

"I'll go and talk to him. Bank managers often mean less than they say." Since this joint account with Donald was the first banking account I ever possessed, I had to admit Donald had more experience than I had.

"But surely we needn't go the whole hog like that?" I protested. "You can't mean cash absolutely no cheques at all?"

"Yes, darling. Knowing us—you and me—it's got to be all or nothing. We're no good at cutting our coats to suit our cloth; and it's time we taught ourselves a lesson."

"But what about money for shopping? The children must have—"

Then the girl at the exchange said, "Three minutes." I had no more shillings to put in the box. She gave us just long enough for me to hear Donald saying, "We'll have to scratch for it. Good luck, darling." Then she cut us off.

Back at the farmhouse I told Julie about our desperate state.

"All you have to do," she said, "is to sell something."

Next day I walked to the village with a suitcase, and took the bus into Cheltenham. There I sold, for no coupons, the new curtains I made for St. John's Wood and my maternity dress. I sold some books, my silver powder-compact, some child-ish jewellery, and a little collection of vinaigrettes I had been making for years. Even I knew that I got only about one twelfth of their value, discounting their sentimental value to me. Then I went to the local newspaper office and wrote out an advertise-ment. *Paying Guests welcomed for farmhouse holidays. 3 gns. inclusive.*

I went home with the unbalanced feeling of far more loose cash in my pockets that I had had for months. It seemed a pity to send it to the bank, to be swallowed up in the pit of our over-draft: so I put it in my stocking-drawer, except for some I sent to Donald, who was now, I felt, dependent on me for cash.

I was further mollified by a letter next morning from Donald. He praised me for my courage in having chosen the austere way out. He mentioned too that he had given up smoking, beer, and breakfast.

Spurred on by Donald's self-denial, I bicycled fourteen miles to some strawberry fields, where I had heard casual labour was in demand. Except that we lived for a period at the farmhouse on the most delicious strawberries, I doubt whether I made much profit out of this venture.

I looked round the house to see what else I could sell. The only things not in daily use were the baby-clothes I had made by hand with such loving care. I washed and starched them, together with Marian's Honiton lace christening-gown and some charming old-fashioned lace dresses Donald and I had worn as babies. I hardened my heart and packed them in the suitcase, ready for Cheltenham next week. Several times I opened the suitcase and peeped in, and once even took some clothes out.

"Don't be a fool," said Julie, catching me with them. "You're just asking for trouble. And another baby at this moment wouldn't help. Put them back in the chest for after the war."

Perhaps I could make a new set and sell it. But these had taken months and months to finish, and the material had not been cheap. If I sewed, I must think of something made from small scraps of material, something never seen now in the shops. Dolls! Marian had never seen one in a shop. I made all her dolls for her. Now I would make them to sell.

I burned much midnight oil making those dolls, and dressed them all differently, to the delight of Marian and James. Julie painted their faces; and I sold the first dozen to a fancy shop for two guineas.

But each doll took eight hours to make: and I reluctantly had to face the hard fact that I was earning only fourpence-three-farthings an hour, even less than I earned as a fruit-picker.

I threw myself into a violent orgy of saving, to the great discomfort of Julie and the children. I saved on paraffin and candles and matches and hot water and tea-leaves. I simmered pea-pods into a disgusting soup. I cooked nettles for dinner and tried to make our own butter, but only succeeded in turning the cream off our milk sour, so it was wasted. Such tinned foods as our ration-points permitted, I shut away in the store-cupboard with the quarter-bottle of brandy for faints.

Then I set myself such horrible tasks as sewing new neck-bands on Donald's dress shirts, which he had been wearing, softened down, since clothes-rationing began.

Donald arrived for a depressing week-end, with no pleasant trip through the long grass to the Three Doves for a glass of beer, no Sunday joint, and only the companionship of a spouse irritated into a state of dull muttering by her needle continually sticking or breaking in the collar-band of his evening shirt.

Donald tried to jolly me along with mock-philosophical phrases about the compensations of the poor. We sat in front of the funeral black of the unlighted coal in our parlour fireplace, with nothing to look forward to but supper of boiled potatoes and spam of unknown animal origin.

A limping step in the haunted passage made me put down the shirt. Donald's mouth dropped open in listening expectation.

"The staff colonel," I whispered.

Before our visitor had time to come into the room, Donald was down on his knees putting a match to the fire, and I was running down the passage to the store-cupboard. I pulled out our most closely hoarded tin of peas and another of bully beef. I put the brandy for faints and some glasses on a tray for Donald to fetch, and called to Julie to come down from her baby as soon as she could.

I drained the half-boiled potatoes and pushed them into the oven with half a week's fat ration. Julie found me laying the table.

"Let's have more candles," I said happily. "They look so pretty on the table."

"Well, really," said Julie, pretending to scold. "You two! You're the limit. Here you are, supposed to be living from hand to mouth with nothing more in the kitty, suddenly giving a dinner party with candles to look pretty. Pea-pod soup to you!"

"But we couldn't *not*," I said, "with everybody going to France. It might be our last chance."

"When it is your last chance to give a party, then things will start looking black," Julie said.

A furry head looked in at the window. It was Hank's. He handed in his inevitable bottle.

"Who told you?" he asked.

"Told me what?"

"That this might be our last chance."

"Oh," I said, understanding. "I see, so you're going, are you?"

"I haven't said a word."

When we went into the parlour, I noticed an unusual air of relief about the conversation. The General arrived; and during the evening several more officers we had made friends with looked in. There could not have been a clearer good-bye, had troop-movements been a free topic.

It was a good party. Hank was the last to go. In the farmyard a young pig blocked his way. Hank got out and the pig moved off. In a youthful burst of exuberance Hank chased it with best quality Boston hunting cries. Poor old Hank, he was killed within three days of reaching France.

Next morning Donald went back to London. I was surprised, as I walked past the Manor on my way home from seeing him off at the bus stop, to notice that the American vehicles were still all there. Somehow we had got the impression that the divisional headquarters would steal away in the night.

I told Julie when I got back.

"H'm," she said. "And I expect we'll have a lot more last-chance parties before they go."

* * * * *

At five next morning somebody came into my room. This time it was not Lucy. I opened my sleepy eyes again and looked more closely. It was an American soldier in his battle helmet; but I did not recognise him. Then I remembered that he was a driver, who sometimes drove the General. I had never known his name.

He stood looking at me from the end of my bed.

"This is it," he said. "We're off."

"Oh?" I said, supposing that one of our friends had sent him with a message. "When?"

"The columns are rolling out now. Ours'll be starting soon. Say, I just had to come. Just couldn't go into baddle without you knowing what I think about you."

"Thank you," I said, feeling somewhat inadequate and wondering if he thought I was like his mother.

"How'd you like to see us go?" he offered. "I can take you along right now."

"No, thank you," I said. "I'm asleep." I shut my eyes to prove it. "Good-bye."

"Just hadda let you know. That's all."

Clearly I had disappointed him. I should have leapt up and dressed and climbed on to the pillion of his motor bicycle and bumped over the fields to see the Americans go.

I could hear his machine outside, spluttering into an explosive start.

Perhaps I was being rather unfriendly. If he felt like that, what about the others we knew better? I got out of bed and looked round for some slacks. I dressed and dragged a comb through my hair and a sponge across my face. I went downstairs to my bicycle and found that both tyres were flat. The grass was heavy with dew as I set out on foot.

I reached the road below the Manor and climbed up on to the stone wall. The tanks and the jeeps and the staff cars and the motor bicycles and the trucks and the ambulances were moving slowly out of the gate and up the road and over the hill. A military column is always a stirring sight; but now, so soon after dawn, with the mist rising above the hedges, knowing that our friends in this column were really off to war, I found myself more moved than I could have believed possible over such a scene.

The staff colonel, erect in a tank, saw me and saluted.

The General saw me from his staff car and kissed his hand. Hank, busy moving his equipment about in the back of a jeep, saw me and waved frantically, signing towards one bulging pocket.

Soon nothing was left but the raised dust mingling with the morning mist, and a tangle of wheel-marks in the Manor park. I got down from the wall and started to walk slowly back.

A sound which made me wonder whether the flying bombs, which our guests described so vividly, had reached us, came from behind me and made me jump to the side of the road. It was the G.I. who had woken me up.

"Hop on," he said. "I'll take you back."

I climbed on to the cushion behind him and clasped him round the waist. We must have touched sixty as we bounced over the cart-track, leaping from the motor bicycle like trout from a stream.

"Aren't you going with the others?" I asked, when he set me down.

"Sure. I'll catch them up. I just wanted you to know what I thought."

He did not offer me his hand to shake; and I felt the interview needed rounding off. I leaned forward and lightly kissed his cheek.

"Good luck!" I said.

"Oh boy!" he grinned, evidently much impressed by the gesture.

He revved up his machine, and, in a cloud of dust and flying divots, roared out of the farmyard to catch up the column he was supposed to be guarding.

I still did not know what he thought.

18

THE POSTMAN never brought his bicycle across the fields to the farmhouse if anyone else was going that way. But today, from my bedroom window, I could see him labouring along with great purpose. That might mean a London postmark, with the chance in his mind of being able to witness our reception of further news of destruction and a possible sudden death or two. He was a relation of the cowman's wife, and also fed his soul upon misfortune.

Julie shouted to me from the back door to come down quickly. The postman was leaning across his bicycle, his little old eyes bright with the prospect of sorrow revealed.

"Thirty-seven, thirty-eight, thirty-nine," Julie was counting. She handed me a great armful of letters.

"Creditors!" said the postman, shaking his gnarled old head with satisfaction. "I know. And you'll have to find a way to pay them. But how?" He kicked his leg over his back wheel and trundled triumphantly off.

"Answers to the advertisement!" I told Julie, carrying them into the kitchen.

Together we tore them open and read of the wives, the mothers, the aunts, the uncles, the whole families who wanted to come to us for a holiday.

"Whatever did you put in it?" Julie asked. "You must have promised them all the trimmings of a bank holiday at Blackpool."

"I didn't. I simply said it was a farmhouse."

"So that's it. Starved townsfolk sniffing butter and eggs and hams and clotted cream. If only they knew. Spam and pea-pod soup!"

"We can give them the tops off the milk."

"What with?"

"We can bus into Cheltenham and buy some fruit."

"What with?"

"With what they pay us with."

"How about eggs?"

"Yes, we must give them eggs. I know! The cracked ones from the packing-station the tank boys told us about."

"They had to pay black-market prices."

"Anyway, what does it matter? We don't mind if they never come again. It's their fault if they've read all that grub into the advertisement."

The cowman's wife, tipped off by her relation, turned up to find us surrounded by torn envelopes, with which Marian and James began to pelt each other as she entered.

"Had some letters by the post then?" the cowman's wife observed, leaning on the long-handled shovel as though it were a croquet mallet.

"That's right," was all she learned from us about the letters.

"My husband, he don't eat cheese," she changed the subject to her favourite grouse, which always opened with these words, while her eyes would miss nothing. Her tone implied that it was our fault that agricultural labourers had been granted an extra ration of cheese, and her husband didn't eat it. This time we let her go on.

"Doesn't he?" said Julie. "Now that's funny, because mine does—any old cheese. Give him a bit of mouse-trap and he'll be happy for hours."

After she had gone we weeded out enough possibles from the letters to last until the end of the summer. Then I started to answer the others, or such of them as had enclosed a stamped and addressed envelope for reply, which were the majority. I was still answering them when the postman turned up with a unique second post. This time there were so many letters, he brought them in a sack and emptied them contemptuously on to the kitchen table.

"They've all found your address same day," he said with relish.

"It'd take weeks to answer all these," I said, horrified.

"They've nearly all got stamped envelopes inside," said Julie, ripping them open.

"We'll just take out the envelopes and put them back in the post."

"That won't get anyone anywhere. They'll think we've forgotten to put a letter in, and they'll write again."

"Oh, dear!"

"Don't be so pious."

"What d'you mean?"

"We could live on these stamps till the lodgers arrive."

We did.

* * * * *

As our lodgers for the first fortnight, we picked out a family from the Black Country. They looked quite nice on paper. ("But so do we," said Julie cheerfully.) Mother and father and the three children would all fit into one large room.

They wrote back saying they would also bring Auntie, Hubby's Young Brother-in-Law, and maybe Grandma—it'd do her good. They would like reduced prices, please, for quantity.

In due course they arrived in a trades van, which disgorged them and their luggage, and their bicycles. Strung about them were electric fires, electric kettles, an electric razor, and a radiogram. The van drove away.

"Talk about pots and pans," said Julie from the kitchen window: and "The Pots and Pans" they were to us throughout their stay.

Our welcome was received without enthusiasm when we revealed, as gently as we could, that we had no electricity.

"I don't know what Auntie'll do about her night tea, I'm sure," said the mother, who was already prepared for the fun, wearing shorts—fully-cut but filled.

"Where's the sea, Mum?" one of the three small boys clamoured.

"There's a stream at the bottom of the orchard," I offered him, invitingly.

"Kid's stuff!" he sniffed. "I wanta go paddling in the sea."

"Wait till after tea," Mum said, shaking me badly. As far as I was concerned, it *was* after tea. Never mind, they should have some tea.

"Which way's the promenade?" asked the mother.

"The what?"

"Or don't they have one here? I know some of these out-of-the-way places go straight down to the beach, but personally I prefer a promenade."

"I'm afraid there isn't any sea here," I said as kindly as I could, although I felt like adding, "and if you'd looked at your map before you came you'd have seen there wasn't any for sixty miles, and, even when you reach the sea, there's hardly a stretch left round Great Britain that isn't barbed-wired and dragon-toothed and likely to blow even a rabbit sky-high, if it ventured within a mile of low tide."

"You won't give me fish for my tea, will you?" said one of the little boys. "I can't stand fish."

I had no intention of giving him fish. A few slices of bread and marge was what I had in mind. However, as high tea seemed to be in his, I did a quick fry-up.

Next morning Julie and I were up early preparing a big breakfast. The Pots and Pans had very much bigger appetites than we had scheduled for. We fed our own children and hurried them into the garden, and then laid places for the visitors.

None of the Pots and Pans descended before eleven, by which time the bacon (our ration) and eggs (cracked black-market) were cold and congealed.

The little boys were nicer than they looked, and played happily with Marian and James in the garden. Each had a magnificent brightly painted bicycle, though none of them had yet learned how to ride. Marian got down to trying to teach them by a special method of her own. She lay a bicycle on its side on the grass and showed them how to get on it, unembarrassed by the problems of balance.

The parents, Auntie, Hubby's Young Brother-in Law, and Grandma, deprived of their promenade, did not even try to be happy, though the weather was beautiful and the countryside never more enchanting. You could see the day dragging for them.

Next morning Julie and I thought we could make them at any rate a little more at home by leaving the eggs and bacon on the table for them to cook when they chose to come down for breakfast. But we were wrong.

Soon after lunch the mother came to tell me she had received a telegram saying they must all go home at once. No telegram or anything else could possibly reach the house without everybody knowing. But I understood her meaning.

"They might at least have had the ingenuity to get themselves to the village, and send a telegram to themselves," said Julie.

But a little later they must have got themselves to the village to telephone for the trade-van, because it turned up after tea. The Pots and Pans, with all their paraphernalia clanking about them, climbed in, pulling Grandma up after them. The mother came to pay the bill.

"It'll just be for the two nights," she said. "And I've deducted for Roderick not eating his tea the first evening."

He ate it today, I could have reminded her: he ate enough for three Rodericks. But I took the money with a grateful smile.

"Thank you so much," I said.

"Count it," said Mrs. Pots and Pans aggressively. I did. But, being so new to business, I made no complaint.

"Didn't you expect us to pay for the whole fortnight?" she said.

"Not if you only stayed for two nights."

"It's usual to pay for all what you've booked for," she told me. "But *I'm* not going to. No, I'm not. I can understand there being no seaside: but no pickles on the table, that's something you can do something about. And fancy having to cook your own breakfast on holiday! And there's a lot of other things what I won't mention—good day!"

She stumped out with as much dignity as her shorts would allow, and then, with less dignity, submitted herself to being hauled up beside Grandma.

Still clutching our small first earnings, Julie and I danced a war dance of delight at their departure.

"Now what?" said Julie. "That won't keep us and Donald till the next lot come."

"We'd better fish some out of the waste-paper basket to fill the gap."

"What about the one whose letter you liked from Cheltenham? She sounded better. But keep your fingers crossed."

"Yes, I'll ring her up."

Mrs. Berkshire with her husband, her adopted son, and her baby grandson arrived next day. They were darlings; but we did not discover this at first.

We put pickles on the table and cooked the breakfast; but I could see Mrs. Berkshire's eye roving round the unwashed dishes in the sink as she sat at the table. I could see her exchange glances with her husband as I picked up Choopy's saucer from the floor, held it under the tap, and slid it under her cup.

I met Julie in the dairy, where we had taken to leaving the milk in pans at night to skim for the lodgers' breakfast.

"D'you think they'll leave too?" I asked Julie, as I skimmed a drowned mouse out with the cream.

"Oh, poor little thing!" said Julie. "Yes, I think they might. I saw her showing him a hole in her pillow-case."

"Mm. And there were all those things the Pots and Pans couldn't mention. Maybe this lot will."

The postman heard our voices and brought in a letter and slapped it down on the slate slab.

"It's from your landlord's wife," he said, drawing back to watch the effect. "I know the postmark and the writing on the outside. She often give me a bundle of letters what she wrote. *Bills what she paid at once!*"

I waited for him to go before I opened the letter.

"Quick, Julie!" I almost screamed. "She's coming over today to see everything's all right. We must hide them."

"Hide what?"

"The lodgers. She sounds terribly fussy. She's sure to object to lodgers."

"She'll probably look in all the cupboards."

"Anyhow, could we make them stay in a cupboard?" We looked round to see Mrs. Berkshire standing in the doorway.

"Your voices, dear," she said, "carry across into the kitchen from this place as though it was a sounding-board. I'm afraid I heard everything you said."

I put my hand over the dead mouse, pretending I was leaning on the slab.

"No, we're not leaving, though I thought we would for the first half-day. But we're not going to be shut in a cupboard either. My husband and I have a feeling you haven't been in the business long. You haven't, have you?"

"No, you're our second lot."

"And the first walked out?" she suggested.

"Yes."

"Well, I'm not surprised. At first I thought you were deliberately doing us down. Then it dawned on me you just didn't know the ropes. I was born into the business. It's a guest-house I'm having a holiday from."

"Oh!" Julie and I both exclaimed.

"Not a bit like this, though. I'd never dare give my guests vegetables out of the saucepan, or expect them to eat in the kitchen or make their own beds. But you can. You can get away with it—you think. It's like going on an adventure—a bit rough, something of a picnic—but worth every penny of three guineas a week, if you've got the wit to see the spirit of the thing. Is that the idea?"

"It's something you wouldn't see even on the pictures," her husband joined her.

"No, you wouldn't," Mrs. Berkshire went on. "The audacity of you both! Starting up like this, no equipment, knowing nothing. And the baby in the bathroom, popping up over the side of its cot to say hallo every time you go in to spend a penny. I was so shocked, I nearly walked out without paying."

"But don't our kids love it here!" said Mr. Berkshire.

"Yes, not a toy to play with, but look at them now!" Mrs. Berkshire smiled, and then began to laugh happily.

"Oh, you are sweet, Mrs. Berkshire," I said. "Will you tell us how to do it properly?"

"I'll tell you what I do in my guest-house. But you might lose the spirit of the thing if you changed your ways too much."

"I don't want anyone to feel done down." I said.

"All right. We'll start on bread and butter." We all went into the kitchen, I left the mouse where it was. I felt that to slip it into my pocket might constitute doing-down. "People expect cut bread and butter for tea, not just a loaf and a lump of marge, or butter if they're lucky," said Mrs. Berkshire. "Keep the knife flat so the butter lies on the top of the bread. If you push it down into the bread with the blade of your knife you use three times as much, but they can't see it and think they're being stinted. Of course there's no harm in mixing a bit of marge in with the butter. That was done even before the war."

Mrs. Berkshire demonstrated and we watched her, eager pupils.

"There's no harm either in a spoonful of cornflour with the scrambled eggs," she said. "But use some real eggs if you can, so they can see the little bits of white in it. It's seeing that counts. Never mind what's underneath. But there, you're not like that, you two. You're all what's underneath and never mind the surface. Look at your hair!" She turned to me. "Do let me have a go at it with my scissors!"

"Now, what about this landlady?" asked Mrs. Berkshire, as she snipped away at my hair on the kitchen table. "When's she coming?"

"Some time this morning."

"You'd better send us out for a picnic."

"Would you mind? Really?"

"Don't you worry. I shan't go further than the other side of the garden wall. I want to see what happens."

What happened was that a very young slim girl, who looked scarcely old enough to be married, knocked shyly on the door and asked if we were all right.

I took her into her own garden and gave her a cup of tea and told her how much we loved her house.

"Don't you find it awfully lonely?" she asked.

"Well, no," I had to admit. "People come and go."

"I did."

"I don't like coming downstairs in the night," I said.

"That's because the passage is haunted," she said, quite seriously. "I never dared at night to leave my bedroom even." She shivered and departed.

I hoped Mrs. Berkshire beyond the garden wall had not been put off by this final piece of information.

Donald came down for the week-end; and we had the greatest fun with the Berkshires, and were all sorry when their holiday was over.

Donald showed me a letter he had received from the staff colonel, who described campaigning conditions in Normandy in these terms: "The weather is vile; the liquor is undrinkable; money is valueless; and the women are repulsive. This, to an over-paid and over-sexed American, adds up to bad news."

* * * * *

Meanwhile the Berkshires had taught us enough about the trade for us to make several changes before our next set of clients arrived.

Nobody else walked out, or even admitted that they nearly had. Several Londoners came, and the peace of the Cotswolds after living with flying bombs—and soon with the new V2 rockets as well—was enough to compensate for such niceties as we were still lacking. And the fact that Julie and I liked other people's children almost as well as our own, and never minded how much mud or straw they brought into the house, made even the naughtiest amenable and their parents happy.

Then came the Artists' Colony. We had picked them out long before Mrs. Berkshire came, as being likely to be little trouble. Artists are notoriously carefree about how and where they eat and sleep and live. All they would care about would be the views; and the superb quality of these was undeniable.

"They may not be much good at art," said Julie, turning over their telegram, "but perhaps they'll be fun. Beards and all that."

"I expect they'll sleep in their smocks and sandals."

"Let's bung them all up in the attic."

"Yes, give them all the northern light they want. How many are there?"

"Three."

We set the Artists' Colony aside in our minds until two days before they were due to arrive, when a letter came from one of them making a few unexpected demands. Each required a single bedroom.

"Maybe they aren't all of a sex," suggested Julie.

"They evidently aren't. This one signs herself Xenia Blount, and she says Mr. Partridge must face south and the Honourable Waveney Macmillan wants a wash-basin to herself."

"Does she indeed! I see, it's to be that sort of a party."

"And they require a communal sitting-room."

"Well, that's a bit matier. Where do we all sleep if they want a room each?"

"We bung ourselves up in the attic," I said reluctantly.

We carried our beds and the babies' cots up to the attic and made a camp for ourselves. My bed stuck out into the landing.

"And thankful you'll be for it," Julie pointed out, "with four babies under four waking at four in the morning."

To support the Honourable Waveney's wash-basin, we brought down from the attic an ancient marble-topped wash-hand stand. We put a bunch of flowers in the parlour, shut our sewing things into a drawer, and flicked round with a duster.

Next morning a large old-fashioned taxi bumped into the farmyard. Out stepped three middle-aged people, all bearing close likenesses to du Maurier's drawings in *Punch*. Mr. Partridge was a dignified heavily-moustached man, who walked with a slight stoop and used a thick, highly-polished stick. The

Honourable Waveney was tall with pin-cushiony hair, and her skirt gave the impression of sweeping the ground in the manner of the skirts of the eighteen eighties, though it was really of normal length. Xenia Blount was the only one that suggested art. She had all the clanking beads and bangles of her kind; her straight hair was wound round her ears in ear-phones, and fringed, to match her boaty neck-line and waist-line, in the best traditions of a lady artist. She, it seemed, was in command of the colony.

"Take our bags up to our rooms," she started by commanding me. "We will carry our own easels," she told Julie. "We should like our morning coffee in the lounge."

Coffee? Lounge? None of our lodgers had asked for either of these things before. Julie hurried off to look for a bottle of Camp. I found her mixing up a brew in an elegant silver hot-water jug belonging to the house.

"The customer is always right," she was muttering to herself.

Suddenly we both froze where we stood. An eerie sound, as of a distant death-knell, came from the haunted passage. It was unlike any sound we had ever heard before.

"It's the seven-foot shepherd," I breathed.

"No. I think it's them," said Julie. "I knew they weren't real when they got out of that old car. That's what it is. They're just a handful of ghosts from the past."

The oscillating lament went on. Choopy arched his back and hissed. Neither of us dared leave the kitchen.

"Look!" Julie suddenly gasped. "The washing's moving! It's a poltergeist!" We always aired the children's clothes on a high wire that we found stretched across the kitchen wall. Now this, with the clothes on it, was moving slowly, a foot to the right, then to the left, backwards and forwards with a melancholy creak.

We heard Marian and James clattering along the passage— at least, we hoped it was them.

"Can we pull the bell?" they asked, bursting in.

"What bell?"

"The bell the ladies keep pulling—like this," Marian demonstrated, "with a tail on it."

"Of course!" I said with some relief. "We used to have bells like that at home."

"You can see it ringing," James pointed out, "up there in the passage. Wha wha wha."

"Nobody's ever rung bells at us before," said Julie.

"The customer is always right," I said, moving off to answer it.

The artists had draped themselves about the parlour, complacently in possession. Xenia Blount's feet were on my very special stool, which Donald had embroidered for me when he was convalescent.

"With biscuits," she half-turned to me to say.

On the lawn, scattered about under Rachel's pram, were the nibbled remains of the only biscuits within a couple of miles. I gathered them up and took them to the kitchen where Julie washed them, cut off the tooth marks, and arranged them on an antique plate which she took down from the wall.

"Got a lace doily, ducks?" she asked casually.

We soon decided that to expect the artists to lunch with the children and ourselves in the kitchen would be out of the question. Solemnly we carried into the parlour yet another marble-topped wash-hand stand from the attic, and covered it with a bedspread on which we placed three table napkins (further relics from a distant era).

Normally we gave our guests two courses for lunch and one for supper or high tea. But all too late we learned, from the death-knells which kept calling us up the passage, that the artists expected four for lunch. Julie ran out into the garden to pick some rather decayed raspberries for a third, while I stirred up another jugful of Camp for a fourth.

The death-knell rang a fifth time. We both reached the parlour at the same moment, from different directions, bearing nothing: there was no more food left until the grocer's horse and cart called.

"Just take the table away," Xenia Blount waved her hand over it.

We heaved it out into the passage, marble top and all. Upstairs in her bedroom, Xenia Blount discovered another tasselled bell-pull. Julie and I spent a busy afternoon racing to answer it, and then trying to satisfy her demands as best we could. Her final demand of that session was for a waste-paper basket without slits, for Mr. Partridge's bedroom, to contain his ashes. Julie took up the flour-bin.

While looking for an extra blanket (the Honourable Waveney had to have the one off the ironing-board eventually), we found an old trolley to replace the marble-topped table. We put the artists' tea on this and wheeled it in to them, then snatched up the babies and a basket with our own tea in it, and ran with the children down to the orchard out of earshot of the death-knell.

We lay on our backs under the apple-trees. The babies rolled and crawled about us. Marian and James splashed naked in the stream which trickled over shining pebbles at our feet.

"When d'you think they'll start to paint?" I asked Julie.

"Tomorrow. Mr. Partridge and Xenia are going out together. They're going to ask for sandwiches."

"Good-oh! What about the Honourable W?"

"She's going to ask for sandwiches too. She's going to hire a bicycle and explore the by-lanes."

"One with strings on the back mudguard, or will she wear bloomers?" I said. "I think she's rather a pet. But brow-beaten. I wonder why she came?"

"Can't you see?" Julie sat up, as though stung by my innocence. "She's here as their chaperone. She's obviously terribly romantic, and feels deeply about them."

"*Them?* But they're both about a hundred."

"You don't know a thing about love," said Julie. "I can't imagine how you came by these girls here. It's my belief that those two have been going off every year together with the

Honourable W since they were art students together, thirty years ago."

"Or perhaps," I contributed, "they haven't met since they were art students, and both have been yearning for each other ever since. This is their last big chance, while his wife's taking the waters at Buxton for a dislodged kidney."

We guessed on through the hot afternoon on these lines, until it was time to gather up the fat sleepy babies and the two wet curly-headed little bathers, and climb back up the hill to put them all to bed and start on the next meal.

After pushing the trolley into the parlour, Julie reported with delight that Xenia Blount had dressed for dinner.

"That'll mean another course," I said glumly.

"But it's a sure sign of her love for him," said Julie happily.

"What was the Honourable Waveney wearing?"

"Just a little bridge coat thrown on loosely and an extra string of beads."

The death-knell flung us into action.

"Xenia just wanted to be sure that the bath-water would be hot after dinner," Julie brought back. "It wasn't, before dinner."

"Hardly surprising, since we haven't lit the boiler for days."

"Well, we'll have to light it today. I'll do it while you dish up the rissoles."

Somehow we scrambled through the evening.

Next morning the death-knell sounded early. We were still dressing the children. I went down, and returned to the attic with the news that Xenia Blount wanted a pot of early morning tea, and so did her two friends.

"Can't they have it together?" said Julie crossly. "We haven't got three tea-pots."

"That's not all," I said. "They each want a jug of hot water to wash with."

"What? On top of the bath-water being hot last night? I bet they can't paint a stroke. Real artists don't wash like that."

With their breakfast I took them our beloved and only daily paper, which the cowman always dropped in for us. It was a generous action.

"Wha wha wha," went the death-knell, almost before I had reached the kitchen again. I sprinted back along the haunted passage.

"The toast is too thick," Xenia Blount was dangling the toast-rack from her finger. Mr. Partridge and the Honourable Waveney sat in respectful silence.

"I'll change it," I said, not really knowing what I could change it for. We had used up all the bread on the sandwiches which, as Julie foretold, we were asked for the night before.

"And another thing," she added, this time with a smile; "the newspaper smells funny."

Anything would smell funny, I could have told her, after sharing the cowman's bicycle basket with a bag of fertiliser and a pair of ferrets: but we were lucky to have it.

"And it's very thin this morning," she went on, opening it.

I did not offer to thicken it. But I did take the toast back to the kitchen. Julie split each piece down the middle and re-toasted it.

"Clever," I said admiringly.

After breakfast we could tell it was upstairs that the death-knell was being rung, from the manner in which the washing on the wire lurched. I went up. The window had not been opened wide enough; the wash-hand stand had not been adequately wiped down; the candle-sticks had drips of candle-grease on them; and would I make sure that Mr. Partridge's hot-water-bottle was emptied?

With sighs of relief we watched the artists set out with their sandwiches and paints. The Honourable Waveney pedalled softly away.

"Now we can scrub the kitchen floor," said Julie.

"We can *what*?"

"Scrub it."

"But we never have."

"I know. But you should have seen the look she gave it when we didn't hear her tugging away, and she came to tell us the moon shone too brightly in her room. Remember, the customer is always right."

"Well, if you think we ought—but there's about half an acre of floor."

"I'll do it," said Julie, filling a bucket.

"D'you know how?"

"Of course I do. You watch." She put the bucket down and picked up the soap and scrubbing-brush. "Here comes the lion!" She stepped backwards, upset the bucket, slipped on the wet flags, and fell into the pool of water.

"Here comes the lion," I repeated, going to help her. But she lay there laughing; and when I gave her a heave I slipped myself and fell over on top of her. Marian and James romped in, delighted by the game of wet bears, and lay down in the water with us.

At that moment, with no warning knell, Xenia Blount put her head through the kitchen window.

"There's no mustard in Mr. Partridge's sandwiches," she said, holding them out.

"You know," said Julie that evening, "I really do think I'm right about the love theory. Xenia was quite kittenish just now over her painting. She won't let Party Partridge see it. She's going to surprise him with it tomorrow when it's finished."

"Hurray! More sandwiches tomorrow!" I said.

Next day, when I took tea into the parlour, the picture was finished and set up on an easel in front of the fireplace. It was quite a good painting. From the window I could see Xenia Blount going out into the field to meet Mr. Partridge and bring him in to see it at last.

Back in the kitchen I remembered that I had forgotten to take in the tea-strainer, which Xenia Blount had rung for the day before. I washed it free of carrots which we had strained through it for the babies, and took it along.

The suggestion of a low fleeting shadow disappeared out by the garden door.

I went into the parlour. The painting was on its easel, but upside down. Moreover it had clearly been added to. Blobs and streaks of blue and yellow paint now embellished the inverted tree in the foreground.

Quickly I seized a palette-knife from the open wooden box on the sofa, and scraped off all the paint I could recognise as being superfluous. There was nowhere to wipe the knife except on the inside of my skirt. I set the picture the right way up, squeezed the two tubes I found on the floor into shape, and put them back in the wooden box with the palette-knife. Mr. Partridge and Xenia Blount came in as I went out. I wanted to find Marian and James.

I found them walking innocently along a wall, one behind the other. Smeared round Marian's mouth was blue paint. Smeared round James's was yellow.

"We've cleaned our teeths all nicely," Marian said and grinned adorably.

* * * * *

Julie and I were just beginning to look upon the sandwich lunch as our right, when the weather broke and back we had to go to the four courses again.

Incarcerated in the parlour with rain streaming down the window-panes, the romance which Julie and I had attached to Mr. Partridge and Xenia Blount ran less smoothly. Once or twice we interrupted harsh words as we brought in the soup or the pudding. The Honourable Waveney seemed powerless to prevent this ruination of her dream. On one occasion, I overheard Mr. Partridge cruelly doubting Xenia Blount's colour sense, particularly with regard to trees.

The death-knell no longer rang, it tolled almost ceaselessly. Xenia Blount's demands increased with the lowering of the barometer. She wanted a well-filled hot-water-bottle, a halma-board, a box of pins. One afternoon, quite unconsciously no doubt, she concentrated on eggs. She wanted a darning egg, an egg for her tea, and a bowl to make an egg shampoo in. Julie thought the last demand, being evidence of feminine vanity, might indicate a return of tranquil love.

We were not able to say what significance ought to be attached to her demand for a spanner, "because my bed rattles so."

* * * * *

On the morning of the artists' departure, we offered our visitors' book to sign. Designed not as a private visitors' book but for members of night clubs to write their names in, it had a space for remarks. Mr. Partridge wrote of the scenery. The Honourable Waveney wrote sweetly of the peaceful lanes. Xenia Blount wrote in a firm round hand, *A most unusual experience.*

When the old-fashioned taxi had borne away our fortnight's burden, our release from bondage was so great that we could hardly bring ourselves to dance in celebration.

After the Artists' Colony, subsequent lodgers seemed simple as a summer's day. Then, unheralded, came a letter from our landlord giving us a fortnight's notice. There was a nefarious glint in the postman's eye the day he delivered it. And, I could not help suspecting, had the cowman's wife had anything to do with it?

I walked to the village to telephone the news to Donald and to cancel the rest of our summer visitors.

"It doesn't matter now," Donald said. "We've cleared the overdraft—thanks to your efforts, darling."

"Your privations."

"Pity we're not together to celebrate."

"Soon we will be," I said. "It's funny, you know, I'd forgotten all about the overdraft."

"The bank manager congratulated us on sticking to our resolution not to draw on my pay. He didn't believe we could."

"Cheek! Not to believe your word!"

Donald was against our returning to London yet. Flying bombs and rockets were still hitting the town too regularly for life there to be tolerable with small children.

Julie and I discussed the situation that evening up on the farmhouse roof, from which we could see a sunset so beautiful that I felt it would not matter if a year passed before I saw another. Julie decided to stay on in the village till it was safe to return to her flat and husband in London. We had already heard of a caravan she would be able to rent.

The following day I telephoned my mother. She was most reassuring about the bombing on the south coast.

"As for the doodle-bugs," she said, "nobody takes any notice of them." Indeed, on my few trips to London, I had noticed that, though faces might slightly change colour in a bus or a restaurant when a flying bomb cut out overhead, people did not allow their conversation to be interrupted. I decided to risk taking Marian and Rachel down to Sussex to see for myself.

Julie and I began to pack up. But we took our time over it. This was our summer holiday; and never were days at the farmhouse more lovely than those last early autumn packing days before we left.

Although I arranged to have our furniture put into store, Marian, Rachel, and I had so much luggage that a farm lorry was needed to take us to the station. Lucy and Nita helped Julie and me to load it; and then I climbed up over the side and Marian and Rachel were handed up to me. Choopy, who had become a thorough rustic, was to stay behind with Julie in her caravan. We waved. The back wheels spun round, as did all back wheels in that yard, we bounded forward, and our farmhouse home was behind us.

But not the cowman's wife. Leaning on her shovel, she stopped the lorry on the cart-track in front of us. She had to pass on news that had just reached her about a lady from London staying in the village.

"I thought you'd like to know that them flying bombs, when they cuts you out, you've had them. But it's too late. You can't stay here."

With a grim wave of her shovel, she watched us off her premises.

19

AT PADDINGTON STATION we were met by Molly, just off duty in her air-raid warden's uniform. She had come to help us across London. Rachel had learned to walk since Molly last saw her. Marian had grown long hair.

Some of our luggage had gone in advance: so we were able to fit into a taxi. As we passed Hyde Park Corner, a flying bomb stuttered over.

"You can always tell when they're going to cut out," said Molly. "This one won't yet."

On the platform at Victoria Station Molly stood by us while we waited for our train to come in. Without any warning, the station was rocked by the largest explosion I had ever heard.

"That's a V2," Molly explained, as gently as though she were pointing out a new breed of rose at the Chelsea Flower Show. "It can't be very near. There isn't any dust."

Our train failed to come in on time; and ten minutes later another explosion shook us. It was followed by the thunder of tumbling masonry.

"That can't be very near either," Molly said blithely, as clouds of dust rose like thick smoke just outside the station.

"Why can't it be?" I asked, not without uneasiness.

"Because we're still here."

The loud-speakers announced that our train was drawing in to another platform. We went across and got in it. Soon, very slowly, it creaked out of the station, moving as though experimentally over many temporary lines. The devastation since I last travelled that way had increased greatly. Flying bombs and V2s had left great ugly sockets in the already badly mauled suburbs.

My mother met us with her car. It was the longest time in my life I had been away from her. Three flying bombs chugged over as she drove us to the rectory.

"Oh, but you ought to see the fighters tipping them up!" she said with pride and apparent enjoyment. "It's great fun. They've got anti-aircraft guns all along the beach, almost shoulder to shoulder—of course I shouldn't be telling you this. The doodle-bugs come over regularly every six minutes when they're on form. First the guns pot at them. If they don't bring them down, they pass on into a fighter area. Then further inland there's another anti-aircraft area, so the fighters have only a narrow strip a few miles wide to tip them up in."

"Tip them up?"

"Yes, they discovered that they only had to tilt a doodle-bug's wing up with one of their own, to send it into a spin and down it comes, just where they want it."

"And I suppose we're in the narrow strip?"

"Yes, but it isn't all that narrow, and plenty get through."

Plenty, but not all, as I could see only too plainly by the new pits in the fields round the rectory.

I could not yet share Molly's and my mother's enthusiasm for it all. But then I was a newcomer to V1s and V2s. They were not my business as they were theirs. I supposed I too should learn to sound callous about them.

We settled down into a quiet routine, which these strange deadly weapons failed to disturb. Every day fewer came. The channel ports were being recaptured by the Allies.

It was almost as though I had returned to my childhood. I took the little girls for walks with the pram along the bracken-bound lanes where our governesses had walked us as children. I helped Marian over the same gates we used to climb to get into the fields where mushrooms and blackberries grew in the same places. Peewits called across the marshes as they always had.

Sometimes Merlin came on leave; and I would tramp through the wet kale with him in the hopes of putting up a partridge. I would tear my hands on what might have been the same brambles I had torn them on twenty years before, as I scrambled through the undergrowth beating the covert for a pheasant. The sounds of his shots were homely ones, and only occasionally competed with the distant mumble of anti-aircraft fire, or the thin notes of the air-raid siren wailing over the levels from Pevensey.

Every night my mother sent me to bed earlier than my inclination dictated, just as she always had done. My sense of responsibility slipped away from me.

My mother nursed the little girls through whooping cough with vigour. I only assisted her. She chose sensible clothes for them, put tottering Rachel into Wellington boots, and taught her to feed the hens. When Marian threw one of the hens into the pond to see if it could swim, my mother laughed it off and gave her a tricycle to keep her busy.

I helped both my parents in the running of the huge, old-fashioned house and garden, without the servants they were designed for, and I helped them in the parish with all its extra wartime activities. I drove those who were sick or in labour to the hospital. I taught in the Sunday school. I washed up in the W.V.S. canteen, and played the harmonium in church while the deputy organist had a baby.

But now I was impatient for the war to end. I yearned for our own home again and to be together permanently.

Whenever Donald and I met, sometimes at the rectory, sometimes in London, we talked about our future home, just as we had done soon after we first met. When we passed uncurtained windows of flats and houses where couples were united, we looked in longingly. The sight of half a pre-fab trundling through a town on a lorry, with its built-in cupboards and bath for all to see, made me yearn to have one for ourselves. We were

luckier than most, but even so, for half our married life the war
had separated us.

Donald said that, although there was still much heavy fighting to be done, allied victory was now certain—and not too far
off. He started to look for a house for us in London. It would
have to have something of a garden for the children to play in.

Spending the most austere Christmas of the war at the rectory
was depressing. It was not as I remembered the Christmases of
my nursery days. Donald was there: and our two children were
old enough to understand Christmas; but all the uneconomical
nonsense was missing for them. We dug up the old Christmas
tree from the shrubbery, and dragged it into the drawing-room;
but there was nothing to put on it. In the country there were not
even milk-bottle-tops to string into spangles.

If Christmas was depressing, the final influenza season of
the war was more so. And it was followed by a cold, harsh spring
with lingering snow.

At the end of March, Montgomery and Eisenhower crossed
the Rhine with their troops in force. Now we hung on the radio
news again, fearing to miss any detail of the advances on all fronts.

As though a long railway journey were nearly ended, we
began to gather our belongings together and collect ourselves
ready to alight. Whenever I was in London I joined Donald in his
house-hunt. I read advertisements of houses and ground-floor
flats. I bought *Dalton's Weekly*. I scanned notice-boards outside
tobacconists' shops. With Donald I explored likely districts for a
"To Let" board on the house of our dreams.

The result of all this effort was the distressing discovery that
other people of our means and tastes had been more prescient
than we had about the ending of the war. Any vacant houses that
we liked the look of had already been let.

Donald remarked on this to my mother, adding that the only
suitable empty houses were for sale—and purchase was quite
beyond our means.

"I know what we'll do," she said, with her wonderful spontaneous generosity. "I'll buy a house, and you can be my tenants." She explained that some money was in trust for her to buy herself a house for her old age. She would buy it now, and we could pay her rent and live in it. We could choose the house.

* * * * *

Suddenly the war in Europe was over. On Marian's fourth birthday, after the last few days of confusion in Berlin, she and I listened to the wireless announcement of the unconditional surrender of the German armed forces.

"Marian," I said, "you must remember this all your life. It's history."

But the reception was poor; and I could see she would forget at once any word she happened to hear.

"Come on," I said. "Now we'll hang out flags." My mother had some paper flags put away in a drawer. I took them out and ran with Marian up the drive to hang them on the trees by the road. Now she understood.

"The war's over and it's my birthday," she told any passing pedestrians. But nobody seemed quite sure the war was really over, except Marian and myself.

"Why did Himmler bite that bottle in his mouth in half?" she surprised me by asking on our walk back to the house. So she had heard snippets of the news, which we all listened to so eagerly! I started to explain about Himmler's suicide but it was difficult, when the only death Marian had encountered was a frozen robin's.

On Churchill's announcement that the next day would be V.E. Day, high jinks were planned in die village. There would be sports for the children on the recreation ground and a dance for the grown-ups. A number of my brothers and sisters and their wives and husbands gathered at the rectory to celebrate.

"I know where I'd like to be tomorrow," I said wistfully. "In London."

"Wouldn't we all?" said one of the others.

"But I am a Londoner," I said.

I went out into the garden to look at the patch of lawn which I had considered just before war was declared. It was a bit lumpy and uneven; a mole had raised the earth in two places; but it was still there.

I tried to telephone Donald, but all lines were blocked.

I knew he would have to work late tonight. I knew he would not try to come down to the rectory tomorrow.

In the morning I got the little girls ready for the junketings on the village green. I had washed and ironed clean frocks for them; and I tied up their curls with red, white, and blue ribbons. I went down to the kitchen for my own clean clothes. My mother held out her mackintosh to me.

"If you run," she said, "you'll just catch the next bus into Eastbourne, and then the train. I'll look after the children."

"But my clothes—" I said, looking down at my garden-stained cotton frock and sandals.

"It doesn't matter. You look all right. I've put some money in one pocket and some buns in the other. Only hurry!"

I ran with the mackintosh to the bus-stop, and jumped on board as the bus was starting. At Eastbourne station I heard Churchill's victory speech. Crowds came off the train from London. There were only two other passengers on the London-bound train. It seemed to be my fate to be going in the opposite direction from everybody else at either end of a war.

All the way up in the train I looked out of the window. There was not a house in town or country without its flag flying for the day. Rural cottages, great Victorian villas, rows of railway-side tenements, however battered they or their surroundings, all had their flags.

In the West End of London the traffic had stopped, and Londoners in summer clothes walked slowly about the streets. Their pace, physically and emotionally, was that of a Sunday stroll. There was no wild excitement, no frenzy.

I guessed that Donald might be at his club, and started to walk towards it through the friendly but lethargic crowd. As I passed Buckingham Palace, a gentle roar went up in salute of the King and Queen coming out on to the balcony. Their slow waving acknowledgment echoed the exhausted relief felt by everyone.

"Oh, how I love them today," said a small red-faced old dear at my elbow. "I come up special to see them, same as the Queen came down special to see me after our buildings went up." She cackled at her own joke. "She did though, and spoke to my neighbour. Ah, but she's a lovely woman."

To my relief Donald was in his club. Combing London for him on VE Night would have been no fun.

"I knew you'd come, darling," he said.

Alan joined us. And, when we had heard the King's speech on the radio, we three went out to walk with the crowds.

As we neared the Palace, the King and Queen came out again. Almost every quarter of an hour that day they appeared on their balcony. We climbed up a heap of Palace coke which was being used as a public grandstand; but still I could not see over the heads of the crowds. Suddenly, Alan, in a burst of patriotism and helpfulness, clasped me round my knees and lifted me off my feet. A number of other patriots rolled down the coke heap with us.

We moved slowly through the crowds to the flat where Alan lived with the Philip Harbens. They were at home. Their habit was to save from their sugar ration and brew their own beer. We drank some and felt comfortably at ease. Home-brewed beer remains a memorable aromatic taste.

The Harben children got up in their pyjamas and joined us. They were older than our own children, and made me wonder how we should manage to feed and clothe so much volume and area of child when ours grew to their age. Their friendliness was enchanting, and I hoped our children would be the same.

Some portraits of Harben ancestors had been delivered from a relation that day. Donald washed them with soap and water.

Alan went to bed. Donald and I wandered out into the night. Even in Piccadilly Circus the crowd showed none of the delirious folly that Noel Coward's *Cavalcade* led me to believe was exhibited on the night of 11th November 1918. There was less exuberance than on an ordinary peacetime Boat Race Night.

Licensing hours were extended, and it was good to see the doors of restaurants and bars and pubs left open with their lights shining out on to the pavement. It was good to be able to saunter in without having to disentangle oneself from the folds of a flapping black-out curtain, which I once heard a soldier describe as like getting mixed up in the skirts of a nun.

By now bonfires had been lit at street-corners. We walked through Soho. There the celebrations had a pattern of their own. Traditional dances of central Europe were being performed with all the skill and seriousness of Highland reels. Foreigners, as grateful for victory as any of us, if not more so, advanced and retired and turned and skipped to their own thin mournful chants. Their old people stood round in the firelight clapping in time.

Donald and I returned to the room in Bloomsbury which he had exchanged for his office floor as soon as we could afford his rent again. His landlady was in a fine state. Part of her back wall had collapsed.

"Today, of all days!" she exclaimed, at the injustice of life. "They'll never accept it as war damage now. Why couldn't it have fallen down yesterday?"

* * * * *

Early next morning I returned to the rectory.

"The little girls were as good as gold," said my mother. "Now you'd better go back to London and find a house."

I took my bicycle to London; and, while Donald was at work, I bicycled round the streets looking for our house. When Donald left the office, he walked round with me.

We knew we should recognise it as soon as we saw it, but for several days it eluded us.

Then one sunny afternoon I found it. In a little Regency square lying below Holland Park, a small house with a balcony and delicate cast-iron railings seemed to ask us to hurry. The windows were broken and the grimy paint was peeling off, but I knew it was our house all right. On a "For Sale" board clamped to the area railings were painted a house agent's name and address.

"I'll come back," I told the house, as I jumped on my bicycle again. "Wait for us."

I bicycled half a mile to the agency.

"Can I have the keys of 43 Pembroke Square, and how much is it?" I panted. I was out of breath.

The elderly agent gave me the keys doubtfully.

"I'm afraid you'll find it is in poor condition," he warned me. "It's been vacant since the earliest air-raids. The damage that nature can do in that time, assisted by enemy action, is considerable. I could show you plenty of better houses."

"Thank you," I said, taking the key. I ran down his stairs to hurry back to our house.

I let myself in. Yes, this was our house all right—welcoming, warming, already happy. A double drawing-room, panelled and painted and parquet-floored, led to a glass-roofed veranda. Wooden steps led down into a little walled garden into which the sun poured. Wall-creepers and shrubs had grown up together, so that it was like a moss-lined box without a lid, through which peered anxious puny roses, begging for care.

Upstairs everything was just as we wanted it. The balcony room was for us, with the night-nursery next to it. Above that, two more rooms waited for our family to expand. I went into the garden again and down some stone steps back into the house.

I could almost see the family sitting round the table in our kitchen-dining-room. Two, three, four children, perhaps more, beating spoons and with gravy on their mouths. Donald presiding, and myself bringing the pudding from the cooking end. This was how home should be.

That evening I described it to Donald. He wanted to know, too, about the bathroom, the lavatories, the washbasins in the bedrooms, and how the windows opened at the back of the house, which faced south, and "How many stairs to be climbed by your elegant legs?"

"Not more than five together anywhere, and beautifully shallow," I said.

"Let me have the key. I'll snatch some time during the morning to give it a quick look-over. Then we can meet at the agent's. You go straight to the agent and keep him in play—hold him from going out to lunch till I get there."

In the morning 1 went again to our house, just to look at the outside and make sure it was still there. The front door was ajar. I pushed it open. I heard voices upstairs. Any ghosts who lived here must be nice ones. But they were no ghosts, only a party of rival house-hunters, daring to look over our house. The agent must have two keys. The voices sounded keen. I went out quickly and quietly.

I bicycled up into Kensington High Street.

Possibly others had seen our house. Possibly offers were being made for it. I pedalled in and out of the traffic, brushing the shopping-baskets of women queueing for buses, as I sped along to the agent's certain that every second counted. I propped my bicycle against a lamp-post, not waiting to padlock it, and ran up the stairs.

A smart, dumpy, but well-corseted woman was sitting beside the agent's desk.

"I shall come in again after luncheon," she said, rising and pulling on a well-fitting French glove. She drew a little away from me as she passed me, as though my mud-spattered bicycling-skirt might contaminate her.

The elderly agent looked up from under his bushy eyebrows.

"The lady who has just left has already made an offer for the property you were interested in," he said.

"Has it been accepted?"

"Not yet."

"Any chance of it falling through?"

"That sometimes happens."

Donald came into the office looking prosperous and with his hat at a jaunty angle.

"Got any nice houses for sale?" he said.

"Why, yes, sir," the old agent started to shuffle his papers in anticipation.

"Good, then I'll take half a dozen."

"Darling, this is serious," I appealed to him. "A woman wearing real French gloves has made an offer for our house."

"Oh?" said Donald.

"Subject to a surveyor's report," the agent added.

"I don't need a surveyor to tell me," said Donald, "that the house has got dry rot in more than one place, the roof is damaged, one of the walls is out of true at the top and will have to be taken down and rebuilt, and there's a jasmine plant growing through the scullery floor."

My heart sank. Donald sensed my mood, and smiled at me.

"But," he went on to the agent, "the price asked is reasonable. The War Damage Commission will pay for a good proportion of the repairs. I know them. Also my wife and I want that house."

My heart soared. Donald took my hand and held it.

"Could we buy it, *not* subject to a surveyor's report?" he asked.

"I think I could persuade the owner," said the agent. "We prefer doing business with clients who do not consume our time with protracted negotiations."

"Would my mother agree?" I asked.

"We can but ask. May I use your telephone for a call to Sussex?"

My mother agreed at once to everything, eager as always for a new project. She promised to come to London the following day.

"You can have your cheque tomorrow," Donald told the agent. He looked at the clock. "I must be off. I've got a meeting in Whitehall in twenty minutes."

I remained with the agent while he made a long-distance call to Cornwall. When he put the receiver down he smiled.

"Your offer has been accepted," he said.

The war was over for us. I took the key again and held it in my hand while I gave the agent all the necessary names and addresses. As I stood there the French-gloved woman came in. I stood aside.

"I have made arrangements for my surveyor to view the house on Thursday week, not before as I want other members of my family to see it first," she said.

"I am afraid, madam," the old gentleman rose from his chair, "the house has already been sold. But we have others—"

"Sold? But this is preposterous. You told me mine was the first offer."

"A better offer was made."

"But you gave me no indication that this was an auction."

"Madam, would you have been prepared to buy this house without a surveyor's report?"

"Certainly not. Nobody buys a pig in a poke. Think of what might happen!"

"The present purchasers are evidently not of that turn of mind," said the agent, sitting down. He glanced towards me and the gloved lady caught his glance, took as deep a breath as her corsets would allow, and turned a rich purple.

"Her!" she exhaled. "And such a charming house too." She turned on her little high heels and left.

"You know, I shan't be able to sell her another house," the old agent said with a slight frown. "You seemed to upset her."

"I'm sorry," I said. "I do upset people sometimes. But don't worry. She'd be a great nuisance to sell any house to, and probably wouldn't like it when she'd got it. Go on selling houses to people who're pleased with them."

Slowly I went down the stairs and out into the street.

I pushed my bicycle along the High Street. There was no hurry now. Home would wait for us now we had found it. And the news was too wonderful to tell anyone yet. I bought myself a sandwich and went into Kensington Gardens and lay down on the grass.

* * * * *

When the sun was lower in the west, I went into a pie shop and bought a picnic supper.

"Two and ten a lady," called the pieman over my head. I took my two and ten to the cash-desk. A jolly round-faced cashier smiled at me and called me "dearie". I shall come here for our rations, I thought. Soon this will be part of my life. Marian will reach up on her toes to put the money on the cash-desk. Rachel will run the sawdust through her fingers on the floor. The motherly cashier and I will make jokes together. With any luck, outside in the pram a cheeky face will be peeping round the hood, and somebody else from behind the pram will be pointing a pop-gun at the pieman.

I took our supper home and pushed my bicycle into the hall and shut the front door. The house seemed happier than ever. I went up to the top floor and brought down the sack of sand put there by the fire-watchers. We shouldn't need that again, except in a sand-pit in the garden. I walked from room to room arranging the furniture, until it was so clear in my mind that I almost sat down on the sofa.

The sun still rested on one pink and black wall of the garden, when the letter-box rattled and I knew Donald had arrived. I ran through the hall to let him in.

He came into the drawing-room. He walked out on to the veranda, looking about him with pleasure and relief. He leaned on the veranda rail and looked out over the garden.

"My father was keen on roses too," he said.

He went over the house and I followed him, saying little.

He spread his coat out on the drawing-room floor and sat down facing the window with his back against the wall.

"Well," he said, moving up to make room for me beside him. "We're home, darling."

"That's what I thought," I said.

THE END

FURROWED MIDDLEBROW

CPSIA information can be obtained
at www.ICGtesting.com
Printed in the USA
LVHW092315300120
645415LV00001B/97